818
KIMBROUGH, EMILY

BETTER THAN OCEANS 77-01808

Better Than Oceans

A CAss Canfield BOOK

BOOKS BY EMILY KIMBROUGH

Our Hearts Were Young and Gay
WITH CORNELIA OTIS SKINNER

We Followed Our Hearts to Hollywood

How Dear to My Heart

. . . It Gives Me Great Pleasure

The Innocents from Indiana

Through Charley's Door

Forty Plus and Fancy Free

So Near and Yet So Far

Water, Water Everywhere

And a Right Good Crew

Pleasure by the Busload

Forever Old, Forever New

Floating Island

Now and Then

Time Enough

Better Than Oceans

Emily Kimbrough

Better Than Oceans

Drawings by Mircea Vasiliu

I Like rivers
Better than oceans, for we see both sides.

EDWIN ARLINGTON ROBINSON

HARPER & ROW, PUBLISHERS

New York, Hagerstown, San Francisco, London

Grateful acknowledgment is made to Macmillan Publishing Co., Inc. for permission to reprint the excerpt from "Roman Bartholow" from *Collected Poems of Edwin Arlington Robinson.* Copyright 1923 by Edwin Arlington Robinson, renewed 1951 by Ruth Nivison.

FIRST EDITION

Designed by Dorothy Schmiderer

Library of Congress Cataloging in Publication Data

Kimbrough, Emily, date
  Better than oceans.

  (A Cass Canfield book)
  1. Voyages and travels—1951–   2. Kimbrough, Emily, date I. Title.
G470.K53   813'.5'2   75–30336
ISBN 0–06–012371–0

---

76 77 78 79 80 81 10 9 8 7 6 5 4 3 2 1

To the General

Contents

PART ONE

Return to France:
The "Palinuris"

Chapter 1

"There! There she is," the General and I shouted within a breath's span apart. The Hacketts, Frances and Albert, on either side of me in the back seat, made incoherent, happy noises.

The car lurched and the General's daughter, Charlton, at the wheel, justified it.

"My God, Mother, you scared me."

As she sobered our Volkswagen Minibus down a cobbled street over a narrow bridge to a broad dock, we were unquestionably babbling, no one listening.

"What on earth is that in the front?"

"Look, windowboxes. Quel chic."

"Blow the horn, Charlton," her mother demanded, and simultaneously leaning across, executed a smart and piercing tattoo herself on the instrument. (Baptized Anna Sophia, called Sophy by her family and friends, over the years and many trips she has earned and carries with no small satisfaction the title "General.") She was the first one out of the car, hallooing as she opened its door. At the moment the rest of us joined her on the dock, there was an answering call that seemed to come up from the water below. Like objects drawn by a magnet, our group moved to its edge and peered down. Straddling, as if he were in a saddle, the wooden seat of a rope swing that hung from a deck above was the long-legged, spare figure of what might have been a coalminer, except that the black covering him from brown hair to bare feet was glossy like tar.

"Too sorry," he called to us. "I'm just doing a spot of painting. Wanted everything to look sharp for you. I won't be long. You're a bit early."

"Now you know," I said to Charlton, "why I was edgy about getting here before the Jaffes and Bob. I knew it would be something like this. That"—I nodded toward the figure below—"is Richard Parsons, the captain and owner of the *Palinurus*. And that"—I indicated the structure on which he was working—"I need not tell you, is the *Palinurus*."

From the far end of the boat—I'm always self-conscious when I say bow and stern, but we were standing at the bow —a young girl came running toward us, smiling.

"I'm Linda," she said and shook hands all around. "I'm Richard's cousin. I've so looked forward to meeting you, though I really do know you," she added shyly, with a smile that revealed dimples. Her voice and accent came unmistakably from England, and her prettiness was just as unmistakably British—cheeks the color of English wild roses, the face a little more round than narrow, the hair soft brown and curly. The figure too was a little more round than narrow, but her eyes were her crowning glory. On a day when Sam Jaffe told her they were just about the most beautiful he had ever seen, I heard her answer, "They were my mother's. Wasn't it dear of her to share them with me?"

4

When introducing Sophy, I said, "This is Mrs. Jacobs," the dimples came again.

"May I ask if you are the General?" and without waiting for further introduction, she said, "Could you be Mr. and Mrs. Hackett? I've laid in a few postcards for you. I know your book [*Floating Island*] by heart, Miss Kimbrough, and with those wonderful illustrations I could put a name to each of you the minute I saw you, except—" and she looked at Charlton.

"This is my daughter, Mrs. Phelps," the General told her. "She was not on the other trip. The three others who are coming were not on that trip either." The General likes things clarified; a blur makes her nervous.

Linda nodded. "That will be Mr. and Mrs. Jaffe and Mr. Wallsten. Richard sent a car in to Paris to pick them up at the Hôtel de Bourgogne et Montana."

A play script would read: "At the sound of his name, Richard Parsons enters." As Linda had done, he came from the far end of the boat across the narrow gangplank and toward us on the dock in long strides, almost a run, and with hand out, calling as he came. He was cleaner only by comparison with the way we had seen him first. That is, he had washed his face and hands. He had not changed to clean overalls, therefore our greetings, though warm and happy, were made at stiff arms' length.

"Everything's quite proper inside," he told us. "Looks just about the same, I think. Do have a look. Linda and I will round up the luggage." He grinned. "I needn't show you the way."

At the foot of the little gangplank Sophy and I hung back involuntarily, and when the others had gone ahead, we turned to look at each other. Simultaneously raising and crossing the fore and middle fingers of each hand, we followed the others inside.

Chapter 2

In the spring of 1968, with ten companions, I had traveled for two weeks on the *Palinurus* through waterways in the South of France. Addison wrote in *The Spectator* in 1711: "True happiness arises from the friendship and combination of a few select companions." We had known that true happiness as we moved slowly and almost silently between Elysian fields of blazing mustard. Over the years between, whenever members of that select company met there was always reminiscence about those days, invariably ending with "Let's do it again someday." If, however, there were outsiders privileged, perhaps unwillingly, to hear our nostalgic talk, one of them always managed to have the last words, and they were "Don't go back, it's always a mistake, you can't repeat."

Now, six years later, we were repeating. We were only a nucleus of the original group—Frances and Albert Hackett, Sophy and I. Circumstances had reduced our number, but we were eager, not to prove our contention that it could be done—we had misgivings—but to see how it would be a second time around.

To Sophy and me the preparation had been both sweetly and infuriatingly reminiscent of that other time. For the original voyage, Miss Diana Shirley of Super Travel Ltd., 107 Walton Street, London, S.W.3, had been our link with the *Palinurus*. She had been a spirited, charming correspondent, but with frailty about specifics. This had been epitomized in my final letter from her. "I am sorry I told you Fontainebleau," she wrote. "Actually the barge will be at a place only five kilometers away, called Samois. . . . I am told you cannot help missing it."

In 1974 Sue Duncanson of the Continental Waterways Cruises, Ltd., 22 Hans Street, London, S.W.1, had become the business representative of the *Palinurus*. I quote from her letter of March 25. "I am enclosing a price list which however I don't think will concern your trip, since you are chartering the *Palinurus*. This is for another one, the *Water Wanderer*. Would you care to have a cruise on her as well? P.S. A deposit of 25 percent as quick as possible would be gratefully received."

My letter of April 2 to Miss Duncanson: "I am unable to send you the deposit of 25 percent that you requested because you have not told me the overall cost. You write, 'I am enclosing an amended price list,' etc., but there was no enclosure."

Letter from Miss Duncanson, April 5. "My apologies for not making my letter clear. In fact I meant to enclose a pink leaflet on the *Palinurus* which gives the prices inside. I shall be sending information on the meeting place in Paris at a later date. Yours sincerely, Sue Duncanson."

The information about the cost and meeting place came from one J. H. Mathisen. His letter stated clearly and precisely the overall cost and that the barge passengers would be picked up at the Hôtel de Bourgogne et Montana in

Paris on September 22 at 2:30 P.M. and brought directly to the *Palinurus* moored and waiting for us at Clamecy. We did not hear again from Miss Duncanson.

Mildred and Sam Jaffe and Robert Wallsten, already in Paris, would be picked up at the hotel. The Jaffes and Bob Wallsten had not met, but I had no qualms about their coming together. Though Bob is, on first acquaintance, somewhat shy and self-effacing, Mildred would find him no matter how many other people might be in the lobby of the hotel at the appointed time. She has among others the endearing quality of an Irish setter. With nose to the ground, so to speak, and, if she will forgive the expression, tail wagging, she will unerringly flush a quarry to which she had been directed, and on the instant of discovery announce it with a warm and affectionate greeting. Sam, with full praise of her serendipity, would add his own warmth to the introduction. By the time they reached Clamecy they would give us the impression friendship among the three had been of long standing.

Frances and Albert, Charlton and her mother the General, and I would convene at the Orly Hilton Hotel and find our own way from there by car to Clamecy. This arrangement had entailed some correspondence among us, but not with Miss Duncanson.

A car would be provided by courtesy of the Volkswagen company. Some years ago I had written about travels in Portugal by way of a Volkswagen Minibus. Since then, that hospitable company, for every trip abroad, has offered, to my perennial astonishment and gratitude, the loan of a Volkswagen Minibus. I am ashamed to say I still have misgivings: Will the promised vehicle actually be there at the appointed place and time? I should be ashamed, because it always is.

Sophy, Charlton and I took the day flight from New York via Air France. In the airport at Orly, after one of the most comfortable and best-serviced flights I have ever known—and because of my air tremors I tend to be critical—we had encountered a phase of French labor that was not soothing. A number of porters sat about in small groups. Interrupted in their conversation, they told us with some asperity they were unable to help us because their working day was ended. I suppose this was their social hour. Since I become bellicose when thwarted and especially when the rejection is administered loftily, I was angrily urged by those resting to search elsewhere for porters. I found several and they were unengaged, but they rejected me because, they explained, they could not work inside the building. I found one eventually who had no such inhibitions; I do not know under what rules he operated.

Because of this frustrating delay it was 10:30 P.M. when we reached the Orly Hilton, too late for information about the Volkswagen. Nevertheless, it was not too late to have sandwiches sent up. We ate them in Sophy's and Charlton's room, and immediately after, too sleepy for conversation, I went to my own across the hall.

In my bathroom I roused at the sight above an outlet of a notice assuring the reader this outlet was adaptable for any voltage. Here was the answer to the problem of my Dictaphone. I had forgotten before leaving home to recharge it, and I knew I would want to use it immediately. I always carry abroad what is, understandably, called a converter. Within a minute my machine was on a bathroom stool, the converter attached and plugged into the outlet; but no light went on. Nothing was converting. The sign above the outlet also said if a special transformer was needed it could be obtained from the desk. I telephoned down immediately, explaining my difficulty and my need of a transformer. Presently a boy who looked as if he might perhaps be in the first year of junior high school arrived with a transformer. He wished to know what my machine was and what was its purpose. He did not know the name of what he carried, nor what he was supposed to do with it. The word "Dictaphone," though I mouthed it carefully and slowly, conveyed no meaning to him.

Realizing my French vocabulary was inadequate to an explanation, particularly since I did not know in English the workings of a Dictaphone, and also aware of this electrician's very youthful appearance, I found myself launched into a kind of Sleeping Beauty story. This was a machine— I told him in French—into which I spoke. The machine would respond and I could listen to what I had said, but when the machine became tired *(fatigué)* it slept and it would not respond to me at all. Therefore it had to be revived, reborn, and this could only be done with another machine such as the one he carried. Once it was reborn over the night, it became animated, alive and responsive.

My audience was spellbound. I think perhaps he saw himself in the role of Prince Charming, awakening by his machine my Sleeping Beauty, because with quite a grandiloquent gesture he plugged in his instrument. Immediately blue sparks went off in every direction and with considerable noise. This scared us both so much he was reluctant to touch the plug again until I shamed him into it. I would not have laid *my* hand on it. Backing to the door without his contraption, he said, reproachfully, without a doubt this required the service of an electrician, which to me had seemed likely in the first place.

Some time after his departure there was again a knock on my door. This time it was a man perhaps two years the senior of the first visitor. I did not go into the Sleeping Beauty story with him; he seemed not to require it. He simply looked at my apparatus, attached it to the machine the boy had left, firmly inserted the plug upside down from the way junior had inserted it. There was no noise, no blue sparks. My Sleeping Beauty and I had a quiet night. When spoken to the next morning for testing, Beauty responded without trace of fatigue.

At sight of a croissant on my breakfast tray, I knew that as long as I was in France I would follow a slogan my sister-in-law once coined. "Throw abandon to the winds." There would be no tiresome calorie counting.

Fortified by my decision and the breakfast, I telephoned to the desk to ask if *"par hasard"* a Volkswagen had been delivered for me, and while the clerk said to wait a little minute while he inquired, I thought dismally "by hazard" a Volkswagen would probably not be there. I had been assured it would be and I had assured my friends of this, and on every other trip a Volkswagen offered had been provided. Nevertheless, at this moment of every voyage in which I have involved dear companions, I am up to my neck in a slough of despond. Entire responsibility is mine—the boat, the countryside through which it will pass, the car that will not arrive. I should never have gotten into this, let alone instigated it. I could still pull out of it, go into hiding somewhere. While I was thinking of possible places of refuge, like Mexico, I was startled by a voice at the other end of the telephone.

"Oui, madame, the Volkswagen was delivered last night. The keys and the papers are at the desk of the concierge." My voice was the trill of a lark as I thanked him, with the assurance I would be down very shortly.

The General, when I had trumpeted the miraculous news across the hall, offered another plan, her own. She and Charlton would pick up the car keys and papers at the desk, locate the Minibus and bring it round to the hotel entrance. Mother and daughter would alternate the driving during the trip anyway, so it would be good to get the feel of the car from the start. They would be on the lookout for the Hacketts arriving from the airport and would call me. The General, intrepid in most areas, is, by her own admission, nervous in a car unless she or her daughter is driving. I choose not to believe my times at the wheel have contributed to this state of nerves; nevertheless, once I have procured the car and been thanked lavishly, I am relegated to the back seat.

Captain Richard Parsons telephoned me while I waited in my room. He assured me all was in readiness at the barge and a car on its way to pick up the Jaffes and Mr. Wallsten at the hotel in Paris. The driver had been given explicit directions about finding where the *Palinurus* was moored, and we should have no difficulty either. Arriving at Clamecy, we had only to make our way to the river, the Yonne, and then ask directions to the canal running parallel to the river and follow this to the lock. He gave me the name of the lock—L'Écluse de— I could not understand the name that followed, but made no effort to have it repeated, because there would scarcely be more than one canal in the town. Having found the river, he said, we had only to work upstream to the lock. We would find the *Palinurus* moored just beyond its gate.

After that call I waited, reading a bit from the guidebook but too impatient for much concentration. At the moment of my conviction that in the excitement of meeting the Hacketts the General and her daughter had driven off with them and without me, the telephone rang again. Sophy, sounding a little breathless and more than a little disturbed, urged me to come down as quickly as possible. She was standing alone outside the entrance when I joined her. She had been awaiting with Charlton the arrival of the Hacketts at that spot, when to their astonishment Albert from somewhere in the rear of the building had come shouting and running around a thick hedge to the driveway.

"He was so winded and so purple in the face I thought

he might fall down in a fit, and he was so angry he could scarcely speak."

"Albert angry?" I echoed. "That gentle man?"

Sophy nodded. "You'd believe it if you had seen it, and I can't say I blame him. It seems when they arrived at the airport, exactly on time, they discovered the next bus over to the hotel would leave in fifteen minutes. Now, you know Frances"—she interrupted her own recital, redundantly, as if I didn't know Frances—"and how agitated she becomes if she thinks she is being inconsiderate in any way. Well, evidently she panicked then, said they must not keep us waiting the fifteen minutes required for the bus to arrive, they must take a taxi immediately." So they had taken a taxi, Sophy's recital continued, driven by a man who did not know how to work his way through what Albert called a maze of avenues from the airport, so he had driven them round and round, always coming back to the airport and always passing the Hilton.

Albert admitted he had let fly a burst of unaccustomed language because he was in such a towering rage at the stupidity of the driver and the considerateness of Frances. Frances kept praying aloud his wild flight of profanity would not be understood by the chauffeur, and the chauffeur had shouted above it he was a Paris taxi driver and therefore should not be expected to know the ins and outs of the Hilton. What he eventually found was the "out," the back door, and arriving there assured them he could go no further, and frankly did not know how to get around to the front entrance, had he been willing to do so. He had dumped all their bags in the back parking lot, and driven off. That's how Albert had come from behind the shrubbery. He had left Frances with the bags and was trying to find the front door, and us.

When I asked their present whereabouts, Sophy pointed. "Charlton knew how to get to the back because the Minibus

had been put in the parking lot there, so she drove Albert
back to Frances and the bags, thank God. I don't think he
could have walked another step. I heard her soothing him
as they left. They should be here soon."

A large vehicle, fire engine red, came from around the
bend into the driveway, passing a typical French car, a
Renault or whatever make, and I thought wildly it was like
a mastodon passing a Shetland pony. I knew, before the
people inside were distinguishable, this was our own Volkswagen, our dazzling glossy pet. We would not be traveling
inconspicuously. A sudden flash of memory reminded me
this had been equally true at the time of our first trip. The
Palinurus had been so markedly different from any other
river craft we were once mistaken for a traveling circus. I
hoped it would still match the red Minibus in eccentricity.
I have no patience for violets by a mossy stone.

Our bags were added to the Hacketts' luggage. Sophy, as

map reader, General and Director, took the front seat beside Charlton. Frances, apologizing distractedly for their tardiness, thwarted my intention of occupying the entire third tier by declaring it would be uncomfortable and isolated. She must descend from her place in the second row and climb into the third. It is not easy to step in and out of a Minibus. Ascending and descending are similar to mountain climbing, requiring a skirt pulled well above the knees, an assisting hand for the descent, and a vigorous hoist from the rear for the ascent. Albert administered each of these to Frances and me; the General, of course, rejected any help.

We were aboard. We rolled down the driveway the taxi driver had been unable to find, and paused. When Charlton bridged the dreadful chasm between an empty driveway and a highway of French traffic, there was an audible sigh from each of her passengers. I think she was embarrassed, I know she was astonished, because she said so, when, safely in our own lane, on either side of us tiny cars like demented water bugs darting in and out, we sang, simultaneously and joyously, "We're off to see the Wizard." For those of us who have traveled together over a good many years, that refrain has become a symbol of another trip unfolding; we are on our way. The way we followed, thanks to the General's preliminary map study and direction, would take us, she told us, off the main route along unfrequented roads and through villages and towns where we might stop to look about. At my urging she conceded not to find and follow the byways until after lunch. We would go direct to Fontainebleau in order to eat at L'Aigle Noir, where we had lunched that day in '68 when we were first on our way to the *Palinurus*.

Though I repeated this earlier date and occasion several times in excellent French phrasing to the proprietor of L'Aigle Noir, he seemed less than overwhelmed, though he

assured me after each of my utterances his pleasure at our return. We had a light delicious lunch, a bottle of light delicious wine, and two hours later we were on our way again. Leaving Fontainebleau was not easy. Each street, no matter in which direction we headed, seemed to bring us back to the great château. We found the proper byway eventually—one always does—and from then on the drive was beautiful. There were clouds in the sunny sky, their movements making constant changes of shades of green in the fields and woods we ran beside. For the first time for any of us, we saw herds of a breed of cattle we learned was called Charolais. It was Bob Wallsten later who told us the name and reminded us that at the best restaurants the menu will specify its beef served as *côte de Charolais.* We only knew, that first day, a herd, creamy white, standing in a lush green meadow, made a landscape to store in the memory.

We went through a little town, Montargis, that, like the Charolais countryside, had a specialty, according to the Guide Bleu—and that is honey—but we did not stop to purchase samples. From there by Route D-93, the General said, and I take her word for it, because maps baffle and infuriate me, to Châtillon-Coligny, and again we did not stop, though the Michelin Guide says it boasts a château built in the twelfth century, and one can visit its exterior, characterized as a "magnificent ensemble." It was here, so the guidebook told us, that Colette married Willy, but I doubt there is a marker of the spot at which this ceremony took place. We did pause at St.-Fargeau to walk along the walls of a very large building towering behind them. This, the guidebook told us, had been the château of Anne-Marie Louise d'Orléans, cousin of Louis XIV, better known as Mademoiselle de Montpensier or the "grande mademoiselle." She was an incorrigible and outspoken critic who had so annoyed her cousin Louis XIV he had banished her to this, at the time, rundown place. She made of her prison a magnificent transformation. We looked through a gate at broad lawns and through another at a stretch of water with trees bending down along its banks. As we watched, a wind came up, blowing leaves onto the still surface of the water. It was the first hint of autumn to touch us and it sent us back to the car, not so much to be out of the wind, which was not strong, but to be on our way, because I was growing impatient and audibly fretful of delay. I wanted very much to be at the *Palinurus* when the others arrived, and my companions of the earlier trip were sympathetic to my explanation, remembering with me the bustle and confusion that had greeted them. Richard Parsons and his staff had been cleaning up after the preceding trip and had not been ready for us. We had retreated in some dismay at the confusion and gone to a nearby café, returning later to find everything and everybody in place and waiting. I had a premonition this reception would be much like the earlier one and I was determined to be a buffer between it and the new arrivals.

Since I have such animosity toward a map, and it is, in my conviction, reciprocated, I count it sheer perversity that from the moment I said we must hurry, the smooth open road from St.-Fargeau turned into a tortuous, twisting, up-and-downhill serpentine. For a leisurely drive it would have been a happy choice, since it wound through woods sometimes so dense the absence of light made an overcast of deep rich green, with other patches a pale, delicate shade, polka-dotted with sunlight. Grudgingly I admitted the beauty of the route, but railed at its coquettish turns when we were in a hurry.

The others echoed my happy cries at the sight of a signpost: CLAMECY. That was a mistake. The vindictive map had not done with us yet. It is all very well to scoff at inanimate objects' having personal attributes, but I cannot find a more logical explanation for the inability of Charlton and her mother, who read maps as I read a newspaper, to take our Volkswagen to the River Yonne. The guidebooks say, and the map shows, that the town of Clamecy is on the Yonne, but five people in a Volkswagen Minibus on the twenty-first of September were unable to locate the river. As we came into the town our objective had been the specific dock where the *Palinurus* would be moored, but as we drove up and down narrow winding streets, pointing out to one another beautiful façades and roofs of old buildings, not one of us called out, "There is the river." On the telephone Richard had said, "Work your way upstream a mile or so and you'll see the dam, and that's where we will be."

All we now wanted was the stream itself, up or down. Of course, we knew the river had to be at the lower end of the town, but the foot of each precipitous narrow street was a cul-de-sac. With some difficulty Charlton would maneuver turn around, we would climb to the top of that rue and try the next one. After a number of these sorties I begged the General to ask a passer-by for directions—anyone, young or old—and Charlton slowed down obligingly. I knew this was not going to be achieved easily. The General considers asking directions a humiliation comparable to taking off one's clothes in public. On reflection, I consider she would prefer the latter.

The structure of a Volkswagen Minibus does not permit passengers in the back rows to roll down the windows; this privilege is granted only to the driver and the other front-seat occupant. I called out urgently and it may be peremptorily to stop the car, put down the windows and *ask* a group of people we were approaching. The General was tractable and even herself voiced a request for directions when Charlton had pulled up. The response to our request was a burst of laughter from every member of the covey. One lady, dressed in the traditional permanent mourning of the French middle-aged female, cupped a hand over her mouth to disguise somewhat her glee at our question. Sophy was indignant, baffled, but triumphant, and said so.

"You see what comes of asking directions of people! They always turn out to be lunatics. These are probably from an asylum out with a keeper for a Sunday-afternoon walk."

Only Charlton had the temerity to suggest perhaps they were amused by her mother's accent. After a pause no one filled, her mother observed in icy detachment that since she had been assured her accent was as close to flawless as made no matter, this seemed unlikely.

"A sentiment open to doubt," I thought of quoting, as I consider my accent quite as good as hers, but under the circumstances decided not to.

Since the Hacketts and Charlton, by their own admission, speak French hesitantly and reluctantly, the General's statement remained unrefuted, and unaided we found the river. Like stout Cortez, we stared at docks and boats tied up along them. An elderly couple approached us as we sat silent. They were unmistakably a lady and gentleman and almost as surely British, each carrying a walking stick, each wearing gloves, the lady a soft tweed coat and skirt of conservative length well below the knee, the gentleman gray flannel trousers, a dark blue jacket and a yellow ascot at the throat. Totally out of character, the General leaned out her window and asked in English if they could tell us the way to the canal and the lock. They were British and charming. We must go back, the gentleman directed, in the direction from which we had obviously come, pointing his walking stick. We would find the lock a few miles up the river. There was no direct road along its bank and the streets were narrow and steep—indeed, we could confirm that, we assured him. If we would remember always to keep the river on our right and return to it down each street, by slow progression we would inevitably reach the canal and so the lock. That was the way it was—up one street, across and down the next—and that is how we found the *Palinurus*. No wonder when we had finally seen her we had shouted and Charlton had swerved the car. There was our barge, nestled against the bank, and there fluttering on a line between two trees along the towpath was the washing of all the towels and incidentals from its previous trip; on an adjoining line two pairs of pants and a shirt, emblems of our captain. The captain himself had been our final discovery, lowered on a swing from the deck. When we had properly greeted him and met Linda, I said to Charlton, as I followed her up the gangplank, "You see now why I didn't want the Jaffes and Bob to get here first."

A motor horn blowing brought us on the run to the dock again. Panting behind me, the General volunteered, "It's quarter past six." Arms were waving out each side of the car that came toward us down the narrow cobbled street we had traveled and across the tiny bridge, and as the car stopped, the door on either side was already open.

Chapter 3

In the exuberant melee of our meeting it was immediately clear, as I had expected, in the space and time of the motor trip from Paris to Clamecy the Jaffes had made Bob Wallsten their friend. I was not surprised either when an immaculate Captain Richard Parsons was presented, but behind his back I smiled at Charlton and she responded with a wide grin.

Captain Richard suggested the new arrivals come aboard; the girls would bring their luggage. The girls, Linda and one I had not seen before, were approaching us from the far end, and Captain Richard introduced them. The one I had not met was Sylvianne, he explained, the wife of the chef and Captain Richard's first mate and general assistant. By her physical endowments Sylvianne could have been captain of a hockey, baseball or soccer team. She was broad-shouldered, sturdy, with muscled legs and arms, and about my height; I am five feet five. Her face did not suit this type-casting. Though her blond hair was clipped short like a boy's, her deep-set blue eyes and high cheek-bones, narrowing to a delicate chin and mouth, endowed her with a head of classic form and delicacy. She smiled shyly in acknowledgment of her introduction and said in French she regretted she spoke no English.

The girls moved to the car, where the chauffeur was unloading the bags onto the dock. Richard, leading the way up the gangplank, paused at the crest. "There is my garden," he said, pointing toward the side of the forward deck away from us, invisible from the dock. I was just behind him. I saw again a series of windowboxes along the far edge, each one supporting a thin line of autumn bloom.

"The garden is not at its best, of course, at this time of year." Richard voiced the theme song of all gardeners. "But if you had been here two weeks ago . . . It wasn't exactly showy but . . ."

"I'm sure it was very colorful," I suggested.

"That's it." He beamed. "Lots of red." He pointed to the front and his voice took on a stronger tone of confidence. "And there is my herb garden." I looked in the direction he indicated to what I have remembered and learned to call the forward hatch. In my vocabulary it was a round roof with two small doors, providing an exit and entry for the crew. Now one of these was covered with low boxes out of which green shoots of varying height and shade gave the appearance of a badly kept patch of lawn. I estimated only a very slender crew member could use the one door left available.

"Michel gets herbs from here every day," Richard explained proudly. "He's our chef; you'll meet him."

When I said I assumed the hatch was no longer used, Richard looked a bit discomfited. "As a matter of fact," he admitted, "it does have to be used and it is rather a squeeze because, as you can see, it can only be opened partway now. Michel is very slight," he added.

Out of the corner of my eye I saw the group on the dock, still chattering, move toward the gangplank. I hurried to intercept the procession. Standing in front of the doorway to the inside accommodations, "I want to warn you," I began, "just inside these double doors is a platform, a kind of stair landing. There are steps down either side of it to the lounge. The landing is considerably lower than this doorway, so for goodness' sake duck when you come in and when you're coming out. I don't need to tell the Hacketts or Sophy, because we learned the hard way, but the rest of you, watch it"—and I stepped to one side.

Sam was immediately next. "Mildred," he called, though she was not far from him and well within earshot of me. "There's a step down just inside these doors. If you don't stoop, you'll bump your head, so watch it."

He pushed open the swinging double doors, stepped inside, and the impact of his forehead against the top of the doorway was dreadful to hear. He staggered back, asking prayerfully for a piece of raw beefsteak to apply to the swelling not yet visible on his forehead. Frances, rushing to minister to him with soothing murmurs and pats on his shoulder, was supplanted by Linda, who had left the bag she was carrying, snatched a wet tea towel from the wash on the line and ran to the sufferer, urging him to apply it to the injured area. Accepting her offer to make and apply a turban, he gallantly urged the rest of us to go ahead and not wait for him. I saw Mildred put her hand on his arm and heard her say indulgently, "You'll be all right, Sam."

She repeated this assurance to the others inside and joined Charlton and Bob Wallsten, who, flanked by Frances and Albert, were being given by them a tourist guide's explanation of the area in which they stood. Something of the clarity of a guide's description was lacking in the Hacketts' recital, partly because frequently the guides spoke at the same time and then apologized to each other, more possibly because Albert tended to drift from statistics to happy reminiscence.

"Those tables at that side are separate, the way you see them, until dinnertime, and then they're put together lengthwise to make a single long one. Oh, my! Romney and Margalo used to play solitaire back to back, each at a separate table. They never spoke, but one didn't like to play without the other." Since the members of the party he was addressing had not been on our former trip on the *Palinurus,* they did not find this information, I daresay, enlightening. Frances, sensing this, interrupted: "That's neither here nor there."

"It was right over there," Albert muttered defensively, "at those two tables," but Frances is by her own admission quite deaf and did not hear him. "It's nice to have breakfast by yourself if you feel like it, and many people do have that feeling in the morning," she added ruminatively. "Or you can join up with others if that's your mood. But the nice thing is, wherever you sit, you're brought coffee and hot milk poured from big china pitchers, though Albert and I bring our own Sanka. And croissants or fresh bread the chef brings every morning on his bicycle from the nearest village. When you're dressing you can see from your porthole those long, crisp loaves sticking up from the basket on the handlebars, and that makes dieting very difficult."

"There's honey and marmalade and jam on the table," Albert interjected. "That helps the diet too, and mounds of sweet butter. Oh, my!"

This is the most violent expression I have ever heard Albert use. It interprets for him anxiety, indignation or deep contentment.

Frances broke in; evidently she wanted no more allusions to food. "Now you see at the opposite side are easy chairs and little couches. That"—she smiled a little—"is the lounge part. Then you see at that far end is the bar. On our

26

other trip our drinks were made and served and we signed chits for them, but this time the General has arranged to provide the liquor and we make our own drinks—much more satisfactory. Behind that is the kitchen, down a steep flight of stairs. The food that comes up from there, if it's anything like the last time, is nothing short of a miracle."

Sam's voice from the landing caught our attention.

"Mildred," he was saying, "this looks to me like a very good arrangement. You see, those chairs and little couches over there make a nice sitting room, and then on the other side, those separate tables could be used to write at, and I expect those are the dining tables too. We make up separate groups, the way we did on the Irish trip."

"They're put together for dinner at one long table," Mildred told him.

"I wouldn't be surprised if they turned them endways and put them together for dinner," was Sam's answer.

Frances was making little clucking sounds of anxiety about his welfare. Sam thanked her for her concern but assured her he was quite recovered. "I'm fine," he said. "Didn't even need that turban Linda was going to make, but it was sweet of her to think of it; the wet towel felt good. I'd better get my things I left on the deck. I feel fine." He about-faced, and smacking his forehead smartly on the lintel, reeled back against the railing of the balcony.

"Sam," Mildred admonished, "if you make a habit of that you're going to hurt yourself."

Without speaking, he bent almost double and went out between the double doors.

The next time he joined us we were downstairs—known in some circles as belowdecks—inspecting and selecting our bedrooms. There was a wide selection since, as the *Palinurus* brochure reads, "She can accommodate up to eighteen people comfortably"—more or less comfortably, in my opinion—and we were eight.

In the front of the boat there were four cabins on either side of the center corridor. On the earlier trip, Sophy and I had occupied the two farthest ahead and had confided to each other we yearned for them again. Sophy had added, "We're just like the old women who go back to a summer resort every year and insist on having the same rooms each time." With shameless mendacity I told the others we would take those quarters because we honestly didn't mind in the least being the farthest away from the bath facilities. There were three showers, a bathtub and three johns. After considerable protest we were allowed this gesture of unselfishness.

Frances and Albert on the other trip had had cabins in the stern—and had insisted this was their preference. Now, however, Albert confided he thought since there was plenty of room they would like to come up front "with the quality folk." The cabins "out back" he suggested, could be used for our bags when we had emptied them, or, Frances amended, keep in them things we would not use every day but could easily get at when required.

A loud halloo from Sam brought him to our attention again. "Come here quick," he was ordering. We found him looking, with something close to awe, at a w.c. When he pointed to it, his forefinger trembled. Within minutes of boarding a vessel, though he has boarded very few, owing to invariable and inevitable seasickness as a child when he was taken on the ferry from New York City to Staten Island, his speech is immediately nautically flavored.

"Matey," he said, clutching Albert by the sleeve, "look at that head. Did you ever see anything more beautiful in your life? It's automatic, skipper, automatic; no pumping."

"Oh, my!" was Albert's reverent answer. The Hacketts, Sophy and I brought in a chorus of joyful thanksgiving, to the mystification, from their expressions, of Charlton and Bob Wallsten.

Sam explained. "On the *Shannon* we pumped for flushing. My mate Albert here always said you had to keep pumping until it said, 'Brooklyn, Brooklyn, Brooklyn.' Another mate on that trip told me for him it had to say, '*New York Times, New York Times,*' and I followed that one. Now look at that sign, and thank God, it's in English as well as in French: 'Push button to flush.' Now isn't that beautiful?"

We scattered to unpack, the novices calling back and forth to one another happy discoveries of hot and cold running water in the washbasin each cabin provided, a night table with drawer space and closet with almost adequate hanging provision.

Some time later the General called from the top of the stairs, "Time for the shoebag. Richard says dinner will be served at seven-thirty."

As I passed his door, Bob was at the threshold, looking up in the direction of the voice of authority. He turned back to me and he seemed bewildered. "Did I hear something about a shoebag, or am I crazy?"

"Shoebag means drinks," I told him, and he did not seem reassured.

"On every trip," I amplified, "the General is provider and purveyor of drinks. She is self-appointed, but no one has ever questioned it." The others had come from their cabins and stopped to listen. "The groups have changed, but the principle has remained the same. We don't like the dark stuffiness of bars and we like being just by ourselves, so we started the routine in hotels of having drinks in the room of one or another of the group, just sending for ice and glasses. The General brought along the requirement for each of us: dry vermouth for me, for instance, Scotch for somebody else, vodka—whatever the individual requirements were. She carried the bottles in a leather shoebag, a bottle in each compartment. Once I pointed out to her—I think this must have been, oh, about 1955—that at a luggage store you could buy a bag designed just for this purpose. She was outraged. She considered that vulgar, she said, and ostentatious. Every once in a while, you know, she reverts to her native Philadelphia conservatism. So the liquor is always brought in a shoebag, and cocktail time has always been known as the shoebag hour. The other *Palinurus* trip was the only departure from this, but thank God we've reverted."

When we reached the lounge, the General was at the bar, demanding somewhat truculently to know what had kept us.

"My fault," Bob apologized. "Emily was explaining the shoebag."

"No wonder that kept you," was Sophy's comment. "Ask Emily a simple question and you're as likely as not to get her family's and the history of philosophy thrown in. What will you have?" She pointed to a row of bottles set up on the bar. "Richard has laid in everything I wrote him about, and listen to this." She paused impressively. "There is a bucket of ice and more in reserve."

"My God," was Sam's prayerful response. "Ice and an automatic push button."

"On the Irish trip," Mildred explained to Bob, "you could have put the whole supply of ice in a fingerbowl. We used to share one lump, timing a few seconds to each drink, until it melted."

Drink in hand, Mildred settled down with me on one of the small couches for the intense catching up that always marks our reunions. In the midst of it, she stopped me to interrupt Bob in a catching up with Charlton, pointing her glass at him threateningly.

"You didn't say you'd been doing a book with Elaine Steinbeck of John Steinbeck's letters. Emily just told me."

"The Viking Press is publishing it," I continued, "and they're crazy about it. Bob wouldn't tell you that, but I have spies. It will probably come out next fall, and they're going to do an extra-special edition. That's what they think of it."

"You see?" Mildred accused, as if it were news to him. "And you never said a word."

Bob squirmed visibly. "I didn't know just how to bring it in," he said. "As a matter of fact," he countered defensively, "Charlton's just been telling me Sam's beautiful picture *Born Free* was given a royal performance in London and you were both presented to the Queen. You didn't tell me he produced that."

"I'll tell you something more," I contributed. "I have photographs of their presentation. They're adorable." Mildred winced perceptibly, but I was not finished. "Because when Mildred is making her curtsy she's not looking at the Queen at all. She's looking up at Sam. She doesn't give a rap that she's being presented; she's just pleased about Sam."

"Speaking of pictures"—Albert diverted us from Mildred's embarrassment—"Stowe's doing an important documentary; going to be away for weeks. Charlton's just told me."

Charlton nodded happily. "So while my husband's away, I'm here. It's a lot nicer, I can tell you, than missing him at home."

Happily, before this shoebag hour turned into an Oxford Group meeting, dinner was announced, later to be classified unanimously as a poem. Sylvianne and Linda served, and at the end of the meal, at our request, the chef was

called. He was introduced by name, Michel; we had already been told he was the husband of Sylvianne. Our astonishment was visible. In physical appearance the husband and wife were as opposite as a greyhound to a Labrador. Michel looked like a poet of the Byronic type, slight of build with delicate features, large brown eyes and wavy, rather long black hair. He was shy, flushed easily, but seemed pleased by our praise. He smiled diffidently when I thanked him particularly for observing the reminder I had written to Richard, that the Hacketts, the General and I were allergic to the point of being made violently ill by garlic or any form of onion in the food. When I said I knew how difficult that was for a French cook to follow, he spoke for the first time. *"Presque impossible,"* he said.

"Tell him," Sam urged, "my wife and I eat garlic in some form every day of our life. We would have thought it impossible to have good food without it, and we never even noticed it wasn't there." Mildred nodded agreement. "Tell him that," Sam repeated, and Bob complied.

Michel thanked him and retreated.

We were not aware of his departure; we were all staring at Bob. "Well," Mildred said. "You didn't tell us you could speak French like that."

"I used to do quite a bit of translating at the UN," Bob explained apologetically, and added, "I didn't know quite how to bring that in either."

An almost visible mist of drowsiness and repletion hung over what Albert called the drawing room side, shortly after we had returned to it. Conversations began, languished and died away. Charlton dropped a suggestion for a brisk turn on the towpath before going to bed and the suggestion lay where it fell. The last thing I remember was an exchange between Sam and Albert about the pleasure of going to sleep thinking of those push buttons, and a sharp

33

injunction from Mildred in the room next to mine not to be vulgar. I fell asleep while Sam was protesting indignantly the importance of recognizing scientific improvements.

Chapter 4

When I went out the next morning, I thought no one else was up; it was only about half-past six. I walked perhaps a mile along the towpath, learning from a sign we were on the Canal du Nivernais. On my left as I walked away from our boat, I was aware of a steep green bank, planted thickly with trees, but when I came to a clearing I saw beyond the trees a stretch of broad water and realized it was the River Yonne. Through other occasional openings I caught sight of charming rather small houses on the far side of the river. Each was at some distance from its neighbor and at the top of a steep path ending by the river's edge in a tiny dock. At one or two of these was a rowboat, at one, a small sailboat. I came unexpectedly to a large clearing that was obviously a camp. There were small tents in rows and from one of these a blond young man, whistling, came out on the run toward the canal, swinging a towel from one hand; it was the only extraneous object on or about him. We caught sight of each other simultaneously and about-faced so

promptly we might have been under military command, except that each of us gave an audible response, something in the nature of a "Wow!"

About halfway back to the barge, I saw Linda coming toward me. The realization that she was strolling made me aware that idiotically I was on the double, unlikely though it was a naked young man was in amorous pursuit. Linda was accompanied by a small black puppy, who from the length of her legs would undoubtedly grow into a large dog. She was loping up the riverbank, failing consistently to reach the top, sliding and rolling to the bottom and trying again, with intermittent rushes to the canal side and demented barking there I suppose at her own reflection. Linda said she belonged to Sylvianne and Michel. They had found her abandoned by the side of the river, at Dijon, she thought, sometime in April, though Linda had not been with them then. Sylvianne had told her the puppy scarcely had her eyes open, and was soaking wet, probably thrown in the river to drown, Linda said, her voice and her eyes suddenly hard. "People can be much more cruel than animals, can't they? And now look at her." Linda called and the puppy came with such a rush she passed us, whirled around, and collapsed in a tangle of legs. I found it hard to believe, I said, we had not met on our arrival; the puppy did not appear to me to be the self-effacing type. Linda assured me she was very quiet on the barge, sportive only when ashore.

"At any rate, now I have met the full company," I said, and started to go on, but Linda was shaking her head.

"Oh, no. I don't think you've met Fabienne, Sylvianne's sister. She helps me do the cabins and the general housekeeping because Sylvianne really does a man's work. The pilot left and Sylvianne asked Richard to give her a try before he engaged another. Sylvianne is so quick and efficient Richard is free to do the navigating, so he doesn't need a pilot. Sylvianne superintends getting us in and out of locks, and tying us up. She's always on the move." When I contributed that certainly she had the build for it, Linda agreed.

"You would never believe Fabienne is her sister. Fabienne is very slender and dark-haired; actually she looks much more like Michel than like her own sister. She's very shy, but Sylvianne is shy too, even though she doesn't look to be. Then there's Yvette."

"On the barge?" I was startled.

Linda nodded. "Oh, yes, but she doesn't do any work; she's Richard's girl. Their quarters are quite separate from ours, off the little deck in the stern. Richard's fixed them up very attractively; even a rug on the floor." The elegance of a rug on the floor impressed me less than the count of people, including dog, lodged on the boat and yet for the most part out of sight. When I suggested there might be a stowaway, Linda assured me seriously that was impossible, and we separated.

Albert was standing beside the gangplank on the towpath, looking very smart, I told him, in a red jacket and red plaid trousers. Sam, coming upstairs, hailed us as we were selecting a table for breakfast, assuring each other neither of us felt a need to be alone. Sam whistled appreciatively at sight of Albert's turnout and was thanked with an invitation to join us. His own costume was a handsome brocade dressing gown over his pajamas. He had been unresolved, he explained, about his own selection of wardrobe for the day and had postponed a final choice because he felt coffee and a croissant would enable him to make a good decision. The sight of Albert had taken the place of the coffee; he was firmly settled on all blue. Nevertheless, he would join us because this was an opportunity to talk over with me a project he had in mind and was very keen to carry out, but he'd been unable to rouse Mildred's enthusiasm. Perhaps after he'd explained it to me I would talk to her.

Linda came to us with a large china pitcher in each hand, filling our cups from them with the stipulated proportion of coffee and hot milk. When she had brought a basket of fresh bread and another of croissants, placing between them a bowl of sweet butter, we gave little sounds of contentment, but no one spoke for a blissful minute or two. I was particularly glad there had been that interlude before Sam launched his idea. After many years of friendship with him and Mildred, I thought I knew something of his enthusiasms and their short lives, but this was a stunner. He wanted, he said, to set up a little transaction: the exchange of his flat in London for a flat or house in Paris, in which they would live for some six months or so. In preparation for that sojourn he would take a crash course in French. A man he had met at the American embassy in London had told him just where to go for this and guaranteed that at the end of six weeks he would be fluent. My heart went out to Mildred, but with a feeling I must not let Sam be aware of this, I stalled.

"Some people," I said, "can learn another language

more quickly than others. Have you an aptitude for it?"

"I think so," Sam answered. "I speak Yiddish. That's how Chagall and I got to be good friends. He let me buy a picture he said he never intended to sell because we understood each other so well. So you see I've evidently got that aptitude. I'm not sure Mildred has," he added reflectively. It was not the moment to speak aloud of my admiration for Mildred's aptitude, amounting to genius, in controlling and steering Sam's enthusiasms. Actually I was a little uncertain of its success in this case, because I had an uneasy feeling Sam was not going to be swerved, no matter how adroit the steering. Mercifully, by the arrival in quick succession of other breakfasters, I was spared further exchange.

With happy morning greetings to them, Sam left the table. He took from Linda a cup of coffee.

"For Mrs. Jaffe," he explained. "It's all she wants, but she likes it in bed." He waved aside Linda's offer to serve it. I wondered if this attentiveness could be a bit of cajolery toward his project, and was abashed that I could have had such an idea.

Sylvianne flashed past our windows on a catwalk outside so narrow I would not on a dare or even for a remunerative award travel it, except perhaps in emergency, and sidling like a crab.

"She's going to cast off," I said. "We're on our way." Had I not seen Sylvianne, I doubt any of us would have realized we were moving, the *Palinurus* slipped so easily from the bank. It was a moment to mark, as we had marked it on our first voyage. The trip was actually beginning, and we rose spontaneously to express acknowledgment of the moment.

"You know," the General observed—she tends to be informative, "we're on the Nivernais Canal."

"The River Yonne," I added, "is just over there on the

other side of that high bank of trees."

The General put down her coffee cup to stare at me in round-eyed astonishment. I had anticipated this and was savoring it. I know that she knows I am incapable of reading a map. This is not an affectation on my part, nor from want of trying. It is simply that I cannot transfer lines on paper to actual three-dimensional places, and though I know this is unintelligent, bordering on the idiotic, I carry the impression that everything on the map going north is working laboriously uphill and, contrarily, going south is helplessly plunging down.

Once on a motor trip, sitting beside the General, who was driving, I was entrusted with a map and asked to ascertain where we were. After a considerable study that had conveyed nothing, I had looked out the window and volunteered since the road we were traveling was flat, we must be going either east or west. Not only has the error of my thinking been pointed out to me a tedious number of times, but in any discussion of whereabouts I am conspicuously ignored. These are the reasons Sophy now looked at me with astonishment and asked, "How on earth did you know that?"

"It's on the map," I told her, giddy with satisfaction, short-lived. We passed and she saw a large sign reading NIVERNAIS CANAL, a break through the trees and the river beyond.

Simultaneously Albert inquired innocently—and to throttle was my inclination of that moment: "Did you walk much farther than here this morning?"

Sophy had not known of my early promenade.

"I see," was her observation.

Albert was visibly taken aback by the acid in my voice when I told him I had gone farther.

When the camp was pointed out, I did not vouchsafe a description of my earlier encounter with one of its occupants. I could guess only too well the general tone of comments about a precipitate flight at my age.

Frances was the last to join us at breakfast. As she reached the lounge, Albert was explaining to us he was waiting for her because they do not drink coffee and he had not wanted to ask Linda to make Sanka twice. Frances endorsed this, taking from her bag packages of Sanka and hoping anxiously Linda would forgive her being late and not mind bringing hot water now.

The Hacketts carry, in addition to Sanka, a considerateness for others I have never seen equaled. They will go to almost any length either in avoidance of imposing on someone else or in giving credit to others for their own achievements. Their reputation as the top writers in Hollywood they will protest. "We had wonderful directors and casts." Their equally successful years in the Broadway theater they deprecate in the same manner. That their dramatization of *The Diary of Anne Frank* has played in thirty-six countries and been translated into almost as many languages is due, they will assure you, to the quality of the book from which it was made.

Frances apologized that she and Albert were holding everyone up. Charlton reassured her by pointing out this was not quite so since everyone was leaving. Sam at the head of the stairs corroborated this, adding he would like to prepare us all for his return. He would be a very pleasing sight, all in blue.

When Mildred came upstairs I was alone in the lounge and not aware of it; I was preoccupied. Her arrival diverted me because it was heralded by curious thumps and muttered exclamations. She was so burdened she must have found it difficult to see over the top of the load she carried and was having to feel her way from step to step. I relieved her of the top layer, mostly books, and under her short-breathed instructions deposited the miscellany on a couch.

41

She sat down and added her own double armload.

"Where is everybody?" she inquired after taking a few more breaths.

I could only account for Albert, Bob and Sam, I told her. I had heard them on deck talking to Captain Richard while we were in a lock. "He told them the distance to the next one and they're walking it."

Mildred smiled complacently, patting the mound beside her. "That's why I've got all this stuff. When Sam brought my coffee he said he and I were going to do some brisk walking every day, and that's exactly what I'm not about to do any day. When he puts his head in here I'm going to be reading or doing needlepoint or writing letters," and like an irrepressible urchin, she winked slowly and at length. "I even rummaged in his cabin and found something that could be mended. Any time he starts that brisk walking business, I'll wave this. That will melt him." She added ruminatively, "I don't suppose he's ever seen me mend anything."

The Jaffes, I thought, are outdoing each other in cajolery. Where the others were, I could not tell her. "As a matter of fact, I hadn't realized until I heard you coming I was alone in the lounge. And that's a funny thing." I had not been aware of it until this moment. "On the other *Palinurus* trip I got into the habit after breakfast of settling up front there with my notes and Dictaphone, round that corner by the stairs. I could talk into the machine without disturbing anybody because my back was to the lounge, and by the same token I wasn't aware of people coming and going. I gravitated to that very spot this morning without being aware of it."

Suddenly I was feeling an urgency to explain a particular quality about this trip. I knew Mildred's capacity to listen and understand approaches genius, so I had no compunction about continuing. "It's a kind of double image, a sort of walking toward myself in a mirror, and yet seeing new sights, things on either side of my own image. A sort of déjà vu, running parallel with the new. I'm describing into the Dictaphone the new landscape we are passing, talking about the people who were not on the other *Palinurus* trip. I wonder if the others who were on it are having the same sense of an extra dimension, or double vision. My God, how I do run on."

Mildred caught me up. "You're saying what I was trying to say to Sam when he brought my coffee, and I even said the same words: 'I feel as if I'm walking toward a mirror,' I told him. 'This barge could be the *St. Patrick* and we could be in Ireland.'* I look out the window and I see a landscape that could only be French: the rows of trees on either side of this canal; but those yellow and brown fields could be Ireland, though the Irish ones were green. I go into my cabin and I could pat everything in it, because it seems so familiar. I feel sorry for Charlton and Bob that they've never been on a barge trip before, because the second time around is better than the first."

"I'll put that down," I told her, and went back to my Dictaphone.

A motorboat on a canal would make itself heard, but not a barge. I am as unmechanical as I am unnautical, so when I say the *Palinurus* runs on a diesel engine, I do not know what I am talking about. I can hear with accuracy and say without fear of challenge that larks can be heard singing above the meadows, wind in the trees along each bank, roosters showing off in some nearby or distant farmyard, but not a rumble or a staccato put-put from the belly of our barge.

The voice that reached us was unmistakably Sam's. I was putting a new belt on my machine. I turned it off and spun

Time Enough.

around to warn Mildred. She was ahead of me. The book she had been reading lay face down on the couch beside her and had been replaced by a man's jacket. She waved at me, wriggling her fingers to show a thimble on the little one.

"It would look more convincing on your middle finger," I suggested.

"I'll just get Mildred," we heard Sam say, and Albert answered, "She can take my place. I've had enough."

Mildred bent over her sewing.

My sharp cry of "Watch it!" arrested Sam sufficiently on the threshold to bring him into only a slight tapping contact with the lintel.

"That's the best I've done yet," he acknowledged, rubbing his forehead, "but I'm going to put up a sign. Now, Mildred," he resumed, "we've stopped while the lock's filling up. Then they'll open the gate when the water's level with us here."

"Sam," Mildred offered patiently, "I was with you on the other canal trip, remember?"

Sam brushed aside the interruption. "Now, I've been for a walk."

If Sam heard Mildred murmur that she was aware of that too, he made no comment.

"Linda's getting out the bicycles. She rides all the time, she tells me. You and I can leave now and they'll pick us up at the next lock."

The shudder that had gone through Mildred like an electric shock had been visible to me. Lifting the jacket, her hands trembled.

Seeing the garment, not her hands, Sam's eyes widened. "Why, that's mine. What are you doing with it? Sewing? You sewing?" His voice cracked with incredulity.

She could have posed for Patient Griselda or Saint Cecilia.

"Just mending your jacket. The lining's torn a little and

I noticed yesterday a loose button. I'm keeping my Beau Brummell up to top form. I'd like to finish it, but of course if you really want me—"

Sam was shaking his head. "Oh, where's my cameraman? I'll never get a shot like this again. Just hold it. I want to remember the picture. Well, I don't want to keep Bob waiting." He went out, calling to Bob he was coming—were the bicycles ready?

"I think I overplayed that," Mildred said. Holding her sewing, she walked across to look out a window on the bank side, craning her neck to watch the cyclists. I did not join her, but I could hear cries of warning and encouragement between the two men: "Take it easy." "Keep your distance, I'm none too steady." "I'll get the hang in a minute." "Stay behind me. I'll keep on the bank side so I can fall into it."

Their voices faded. Resuming her seat and, with a grimace, her sewing, she gave her judgment.

"He'll either fall in the water or have a heart attack or both."

Sam did not have a heart attack nor fall in the canal. Mildred did not get on a bicycle and Sam never rode again. Over his groans that night as Mildred rubbed his muscles, I heard him declare he would not mount a bicycle again, though only because he preferred walking.

That Mildred should have produced liniment was no surprise to those of us who had traveled with her before. A separate bag in her luggage was devoted to a pharmaceutical supply she longed to diminish. It was not easy to escape Dr. Jaffe's enthusiastic ministrations.

Coming up for breakfast next morning around eight, I was told the General had already left in search of a taxi. She would go back to Clamecy, retrieve our Volkswagen bus and, at Captain Richard's request, pick up laundry for the boat deposited the day before at the village *lavage*. We were tied up at Dirol, across the canal from Monceau le Comte, but the day before had been such a long run, interrupted by so many locks, we had not moored until half-past seven, too late for exploring the vicinity.

Walking about the village of Monceau le Comte, I was not really seeing it, because the roadside was deep in fallen leaves. I do not remember meeting any of my *Palinurus* companions. I think I walked around a statue behind a circular iron fence, a bust, probably, of Lamartine, since this was his countryside. When autumn leaves are on the ground I must scuff through them, and I am both in and out of the present. It is irresistible for me to scuff.

Heading back toward the boat, I realized what I was doing. This is how as one grows older the then and now run parallel, each enriching the other. Part of me was walking along the gutter on Washington Street in Muncie, Indiana, and the pleasure of doing this at Monceau le Comte in the middle of France was just as sharp. The reminiscent smell of bonfires was just as sharp too, though I am not sure in Monceau le Comte people were burning leaves that day.

The Volkswagen was parked at a tilt on a grassy bank along the towpath, so I knew Sophy was back. As I crossed the little gangplank to the *Palinurus* deck I was assured again of her return by the sound of her voice in vehement emphasis.

"Do you realize we couldn't even find the canal yesterday, let alone the *Palinurus?* Well, just try to picture me finding a laundry, and every person I stopped to ask the way snickered at me." Catching sight of me in the doorway, "Don't dare say it was my accent."

"I wouldn't," I assured her.

She swept on. "Finally one of the idiot inhabitants asked me what I was driving; he'd never seen a car for passengers that was so big. But he didn't know where the laundry was. Anyway, I'm back, so we can get going."

We did take off shortly after thirteen past ten, the General said. She always announces the exact time of our departure and arrival, but I have never ventured to ask her why. Everyone but me, I was thinking, had welcomed Sophy's return, but then the voices of Sam and Bob on the stairs prefaced their joining us. Sam was carrying two jackets, the one Mildred had been working on and a dark blue windbreaker. Bob was protesting the acceptance of either. Sam overrode this.

"When you came on board just now you were carrying on like a windmill, trying to get circulation going again. These mornings are cold, and you haven't got a jacket."

"I brought sweaters," Bob protested, "a thin one and this Irish one I've got on. I thought they would be plenty, but I was going to Italy first. I just didn't 'think cold.'"

Sam resumed his sales talk. "Now, I've got these two jackets and I only need one. Matter of fact, I've got still another one below. When I travel I rather like to spread myself. The only question is, which? Now"—holding out the blue windbreaker—"this is what I'd usually wear. I haven't seemed to wear this other one much, but that was before Mildred mended it. Since I never saw her mend anything before, she could be offended if I handed her big work over to somebody else, so you'll have to leave that one to me." He pushed the windbreaker into Bob's arms with a little pat as he relinquished it. "I'm fond of that jacket. It'll look great on you."

Across the room I caught Mildred's eye and she had the grace to bow her head in shame, but as she bowed she winked.

Chapter 5

We were at Chitry-les-Mines at lunchtime. We were having a drink and debating going ashore when Captain Richard came into the lounge from the stairs to the kitchen. I meant to ask him why in converting the barge he had not thought of putting the kitchen on a level with the lounge, eliminating the need for carrying trays up and down a long and narrow stairway. He evidently had an announcement to make, so I let my question go, and I never did find out the reason.

His announcement was that we would be here several hours. Michel was going for provisions by taxi to a neighboring village with superior markets. He would take his wife and her sister with him.

"That's very nice of him," I interrupted, "to give the girls an outing." Richard smiled and I wondered why, but he was still talking. The mines, he said, that gave the place its name, Chitry-les-Mines, had long since petered out and were no longer worked. I wondered what kind of mines they had been, but forbore to ask because he evidently had other things to tell us. The village itself, he said, was quite charming and on its outskirts was a really handsome château. We could spend as much time as we liked because the afternoon run would be a short one. We would not try to reach the town of Baye until the following night; too many locks between.

"We'll tie up tonight at Yonne Lock Twenty-four."

"Yonne," I echoed. "Why, that's the river. I thought we were still on the Nivernais Canal with the river alongside."

"Baye is where the river leaves us. Look, I'll show you on the map." Involuntarily I groaned.

The General, hearing, muttered to me, "Well, you asked for it."

Why, I asked myself wrathfully, when I didn't ask him what he found amusing about Michel taking the girls to market and what kind of mines were Chitry-les-Mines, would I have to blurt out a question that involved a map?

Richard opened a drawer behind the bar, so tightly stuffed with maps and charts it was like uncapping a bottle of club soda after shaking it.

"These are maps," Richard told us, gathering them up from the floor and the bar counter, where the explosion had shot them. "You're welcome to look at any of them. I've got duplicates in my quarters."

The others were moving hungrily toward them—that is, all but Mildred.

"I'd rather look at the place when I get there," she confided to me.

We did enter the spirit of "show and tell" enough to remove a miscellany of books, writing paper and other trivia from the coffee table in front of a couch. Then we retreated to sit comfortably on an adjoining couch while Richard, his audience close around him, showed and told.

"Baye—" he said, "you see it here—is where we'll moor

tomorrow. One might say it's a peak of the canal. You'll notice all the locks are numbered and in the direction we're going they're backward, so to speak. Before we reach Yonne Lock Twenty-four we will have gone through descending numbers from Clamecy, which was Forty-seven. Here at Chitry we're at Twenty-nine. At Yonne Twenty-four, where we'll be tonight, we lose the river running along parallel."

"Look at them." Mildred nudged me. "They're like children listening to 'The Three Bears.'"

Richard continued to show and talk. "Now, when we get to Baye, and that should be tomorrow night, the lock will be number One and from there on south in that sequence—Two, Three, et cetera. You've seen, of course, that we've been going up all this time. At every lock we've had to be raised to meet the level of the canal on the other side."

There was a pause . . . "Oh, yes." "Of course." "Certainly." Mildred's head and mine were shaken simultaneously and negatively at each other.

"Now," Richard was saying, "we'll be going down, so at every lock we'll be lowered to the level of the water beyond."

Fabienne announced lunch.

Conversation at lunch was still devoted to maps, and I thanked God for the presence of Mildred and her alliance with me. Every other inquisitor at that table, all dear friends, demanded to know why we did not feel maps the most fascinating reading in the world. How could anyone plan a trip without poring over maps? Had we no conception of the joy in finding and reading aloud names of far-off places in all probability one would never see? The lunch, like every other meal, was delicious and Mildred and I indicated to each other how deeply we appreciated *this*. Bob said what Richard had been showing them were charts, actually, and the best he had ever seen, and Sam agreed with him.

"What I saw," I told Mildred quietly, "were black-and-white pen-and-ink line drawings with wash, not very decorative and certainly not illuminating to me."

"I'll tell you what I'll do," Bob was saying to Sophy. "When we get to a town big enough to have the equipment, I'll get these charts Xeroxed with a set for you and one for me."

"Count me in," Charlton said. "I'd love to own a set, a wonderful souvenir of the trip."

The Hacketts declined. They adored maps, Frances explained, but they would not dream of asking Bob to take the trouble to have an extra set struck off for them. Sam thought he might like one, but at a look from Mildred said he guessed not.

The château at Chitry-les-Mines is not difficult to find and it is beautiful. Dominating the little village, its acres of green lawn with fields on either side run down almost to the canal itself. After a long, low whistle of surprise and pleasure, Sam was all for buying it. He visualized for all of us the life of pastoral contentment he and Mildred would lead, surrounded by beauty. At the end of fifteen minutes, while Mildred smiled and said nothing and the rest of us wandered about, sometimes within his earshot and often not, he had moved into and out of the estate. Difficult to run, he acknowledged when we had reassembled, since he was not quite ready for the language. Their housekeeper in London, whom they would bring, of course, was Spanish.

As Richard had directed, we turned one way to reach the château, and since there was only one road, we followed it in the opposite direction to reach the village. The château was not open to the public, but we had been happily satisfied to enjoy its exterior. The road curved unexpectedly and brought us to a loquacious busybody little stream chattering alongside an old mill. After the unruffled surface of the canal, it was almost embarrassing, I said, to come upon this impertinent gamine of a waterway.

In my hearing there has never been conversation on a barge trip about a schedule or pattern ashore. It is simply —and it always happens—that once off the boat we scatter, not prompted by a feeling of having been cooped up and wanting to break out, of boredom or exasperation with one another; rather, one of us may see something provocative for investigating, pursue it, turn to comment on it and find he's alone; sometimes he comes upon other members of the group, exchanges tidbits of things seen and what to see, and moves on.

Straggling, some of us converged on a little shop run by a pleasant-looking and helpful young woman. With the arrival of each straggler she became more helpful and more confused until finally with hands outspread and shaking she admitted she was completely *éblouie*—dazzled, turned upside down—because she had not done so much business in a day, in a week, in a—with a violent shrug—she did not know what, as we were bringing her this afternoon. We bought postcards, pencils, writing pads, drawing pads— Bob wanted to sketch. As my Greek friend Gina Bachauer says, "Everything what you can imagine." And when each of us had assembled on the counter his heap of merchandise for totaling, the young proprietor collapsed. Rocking her head between her hands, she protested wildly, "I do not think I can add so much. I am in confusion."

Though he has never been appointed there, Bob is a loss to the Court of St. James's. With gentle authority he took over, soothed and complimented mademoiselle, restored her coherence so that she could give him the price of each article. He added the collected purchases, she showed him with trembling fingers the cash drawer, and he made change. She shook hands all round, thanking us quaveringly, and from the doorway waved us off, sitting on a chair Bob had brought her from a corner of the shop.

Frances and Albert were playing gin rummy in the lounge. I saw them through a window as we came on board. We had not scattered again after our spate of buying, probably because each of us was too encumbered with the packaged result. Frances, looking up briefly from the game to acknowledge our arrival, caught sight of one of my packages, a small paper bag with an open top.

"Are those postcards?" she demanded, and simultaneously, "Albert! Postcards!" Albert, preoccupied with the game, suffered a delayed reaction by having all the playing cards pushed across the table and into his lap. He saw his wife leap from her chair and heard her call, in the manner of one announcing a fire, "Postcards! Hurry!"

That I should even momentarily have forgotten the Hacketts and postcards alarms me. On every trip on which we have been companions they have pursued and found postcards, often in the most unlikely places—fish markets, bakeries and even pubs. Theirs is a distinguished collection of pictures, that when not on loan for various exhibitions (because they are in demand) can be seen on the walls in their apartment. I have never seen their postcard collection, but it must fill more volumes than are required for the *Encyclopaedia Britannica.* At the time of their purchase, before they are stored away, the cards are pored over lovingly, passed from one to the other for reaffirmation of the delight in having found that very special one. Sometimes, because they are generous people, they write on and mail to friends selections from the collection, chosen with considerable deliberation and, I suspect, reluctance.

They were down the gangplank and some distance along the towpath when Albert turned and ran back, calling, "Which way is the shop?" I pointed and he was off again, Frances by that time well ahead of him. Bob, standing beside me, frowned a little, shaking his head.

"Maybe I ought to go along to help that poor girl," he said.

While we were watching the briskly retreating Hacketts, a taxi came jolting along the towpath, that had not the smoothness of a village street. Charlton had assured her mother—who, when not being a general, tends to cluck a little—the towpath was wide enough for a car and so it was certainly not perilous for her cycling, but we had seen no motor traffic on it.

The reason the taxi driver had been persuaded to use it was obvious the moment the doors were opened. Sylvianne and Fabienne came out from either side; Michel on the front seat remained talking to the driver beside him. The girls, turning back to the interior, brought out one by one four or five big open cartons. Looking down on them from our commanding position we could see chickens, an unmistakable leg of lamb, other meats, heads of lettuce, vegetables. Unlike the effete delicacy exercised at home, nothing was wrapped. It was a colorful jumble. Out of each corner rose loaves of bread tall enough to be used as walking sticks. Pointing this out to Bob, I said the reason I had used the comparison was that once in Paris I had seen a loaf of bread adapted to this purpose by an elderly gentleman returning home from the bakery.

When all the cartons were unloaded from the car, Sylvianne picked up the carton nearest her and with an easy and graceful motion lifted and swung it to her shoulder. Bob involuntarily started forward, obviously intending to help her. I do not know when Sam had joined us, but he put a restraining hand on Bob's arm.

"Better not get into that. You can see it's women's work."

"Custom of the country, I guess," was Bob's rejoinder. We watched the girls carry one after another of the car-

tons on board. Fabienne, who could not have weighed more than ninety pounds, handled hers with the ease Sylvianne had displayed. When the last carton was on board, Sylvianne from the stern called, *"Finis,"* to Michel. From between thumb and index finger he flicked to the towpath the stub of a cigarette, then he turned to the taxi driver, shook hands with him and, carrying a small paper bag and a sweater, left the taxi. Catching sight of us, he nodded shyly and moved in a very leisurely way toward the stern, allowing time, I told my companions, for the girls to have everything unpacked and put away. Evidently this had not been quite completed, because he came out again almost immediately, bringing the puppy for an exuberant frolic.

Returning inside, on the threshold of the lounge I stopped suddenly, somewhat to the discomfiture of Bob and Sam, immediately behind me. I apologized and explained.

"I suddenly saw in my mind's eye Richard talking to us before lunch about our stopover here. He said Michel was going to another village for marketing and taking Sylvianne and Fabienne with him. I said, what a nice thing that was for Michel to do, giving the girls a little outing, and Richard laughed. I wondered why. It had not seemed to me I had said anything amusing. Ha!"

Chapter 6

The Eve of our Long Day's Journey into Night, as it was ever after identified, was spirited. Before the shoebag hour, Charlton and Albert went on a bicycle expedition. They gave tantalizing reports over cocktails of a château and rabbits. They were loftily superior to our jeering inquiries about rabbits.

"We'll show you," was Charlton's only concession. "It won't be far in the Minibus from wherever we moor tomorrow night." She would never forget, she admitted later, the day between those moorings.

"You know," she continued, "it makes me realize that for all I've been told about these barge trips, I really hadn't taken it in. Lord knows I've sailed and cruised, but this is really something else, as the kids say."

"Very hard to describe to people," Frances acknowledged, a little smugly, I thought.

"Well, look at today," Charlton continued, as if she were defending the assertion. "I've walked, picked those wildflowers along a bank"—she indicated a charming arrangement on the coffee table in front of her—"I've gone in a taxi to bring back our Minibus. It took twenty minutes. We've spent all day covering that distance. Albert and I have had a bicycle tour. And when we show you what we saw it will take maybe a little longer, but not much, and there will have been a day's barge travel between."

Sam interrupted. He was standing at the head of the stairs. He wished to be recognized in the role of executive producer, he told us. The production was very recently completed; the star would shortly appear. Well aware of the hazards of which they had been warned, they had nevertheless plunged in; specifically, he wished to be exact, Mildred had plunged into the tub. Thanks to his expert directing and background assistance, her entrance and exit had been flawless. We greeted the star's arrival with cheers, congratulations and toasts.

"Try to describe the *Palinurus*'s tub," I heard Charlton tell Mildred, and I echoed Frances's emphatically voiced agreement.

A high standard of cleanliness had been consistently maintained from the start of the cruise, but the instrument for this maintenance had been a shower. The *Palinurus* boasted three of these and one tub. The *Palinurus*'s tub was unusual in dimension and position. The choice between it and a shower required more than the flip of a coin. A shower could be taken at any time without acknowledgment of one's intention and requiring only the provision that the stall was not occupied. For a tub, an assistant was required, to respond on the jump to a call for help. This moment of need could happen when the bather was either entering or leaving the tub or standing up in it. On our previous *Palinurus* voyage the means of entry and exit was the usual one of climbing in, but with a difference. The height from the floor was a little greater than that of a practice bar for ballet dancers. It could happen—indeed it did happen—that the bather was transfixed with one foot on the lip of the tub, the other on the floor, and without sufficient momentum to leave the ground or release the agonizingly extended other leg, remaining immobilized: as my brother, a passenger on that trip, coarsely put it, split for broiling. This was a moment when piercing cries for help penetrated the lounge, even the deck.

The lack of distance between the bottom of the tub proper and the ceiling provided another hazard. Only someone of under-average height could stand up in it. Romney Brent, a passenger on that earlier trip and a man a little under the average stature, rose up from his bath, reaching at the same time for a towel on an adjoining rack, and encountered on his rear an unshaded lighted electric bulb. The resultant discomfort persisted for several days.

Since that trip the only change had been the installation of a movable short flight of steps like a kitchen ladder. Showing this to me, Richard had pridefully boasted it made getting in and out as easy as falling off a log.

Accepting this, I had tried getting into the tub two nights before Mildred's immersion. I have never tried rolling off a log. There was nothing to grip at the top of the ladder and nothing on the near side to hold, by which to lower myself. I had stood on the top of the ladder, the palm of my hand pressed against the wall for support, clamped to it as if cemented. Charlton, responding to my tremulous but piercing, she said, yells for help, had said it was so difficult to pry my hand away it might have been embedded there by suction. With her steadying assistance from the rear, I backed down the steps, thanked her fervently, and God, that I hadn't locked the door, put on my bathrobe again, gathered up towel, soap and sponge, and went directly to the shower. I never set foot in the tub.

Tattletale Charlton on the way from the rescue to her

cabin had encountered her mother and gleefully exposed my ignominious and craven surrender. The General had decided on the instant to have a tub bath. Returning with a song in my heart at the ease and comfort of a shower, I had seen her at the doorway of the, to me, chamber of horrors. Her greeting was so casual I was sure she had been waiting for me.

"I'm just going to take a tub," she said. "Charlton tells me you changed your mind about taking one." There were a few things I thought I would tell later to that good Samaritan Charlton.

With tolerant amusement that I should suggest it, she flouted my offers to stand by. I went on to my cabin and dressed for dinner. We were having our drinks when Linda came into the lounge to say dinner at the General's request would be a little delayed.

"By the merest chance," Linda explained, "I was taking some things I had pressed to Mrs. Jaffe's cabin and I heard poundings on the door of the tub room and saw the door-knob turning back and forth. Your mother"—she was looking at Charlton—"had locked herself in somehow. I ran and got a key that unlocks all the doors from the outside."

The General tolerated our amusement and our sympathy, with appreciably more warmth for the latter, adding, as we moved to the dinner table, she had wondered whether her absence would be noticed before the meal was over.

After dinner, merry as grigs, although I am not sure what a grig is or why it is merry, we played the telephone game. We had played it on the Irish cruise, but since Charlton and Bob were newcomers to this, we explained it, not by turns, with resultant almost total confusion. Eventually, at her own request, the General, silencing with an authoritative hand every abortive interruption, gave the following outline:

On a sheet of paper, preferably typewriter size, the

player, down the left-hand margin, lists the letters of the alphabet, one beneath the preceding, and leaving the equivalent of double or even triple typewriter space between each two. If he has reached the bottom of the page before achieving the end of the alphabet, he draws a line down the center of the sheet and completes the alphabet on the right-hand side of the center line, allowing again the spaces between. When this has been done, one of the players, either volunteering or being asked, assigns a letter and simultaneously starts the timing. In the allotted time, usually ten minutes, the players must set down opposite the proper letter, names of well-known people whose last name begins with the letter given. The catch, trick or difficulty of this game is that the first name must also be given and the whole name listed opposite the letter of the first name. For example, if the letter *R* is the one given, it is not enough to think of and to set down, say, Rubinstein, Renoir, Rodin, Raft. Each name must be entered as in a telephone book, with the inclusion of the first name, but unlike telephone book entries, these are made opposite the first letter of the first name. In other words, Rubinstein is Artur and it must be written down "Artur Rubinstein" under the letter *A*. Renoir must be listed "Pierre Renoir" and entered opposite the letter *P*, the whole name of course being written down. Raft is "George Raft" and entered opposite *G*.

The object of the game is to set down in the ten minutes as many names as possible. When the time is up the time-keeper asks each player in turn to give his names if he has any under the letter *A*. If he has one or more and no one else has the same names, he scores himself ten for each. If someone else in the group also has that same name, each scores himself five, and if more than two have the same, each one gives himself three. When the alphabet is completed, the scores are totaled, and when the names opposite each letter of the alphabet have been read off, given their proper score and approved, the results then are totaled for the highest score. That is the structure of the game, but the spirit of it rises from approval to challenges. These can be vehement and demonstrative.

Mildred's range of painters is wide. Sam's range includes, in addition to painters, Hollywood and sports notables. To challenge any one of these claimants to our hall of fame was to rouse Sam to an oratorical fervor that could have brought to its feet an audience at a political convention or revivalist meeting. He begged us not to dishonor these people by pretending an ignorance of them, because surely we could not be so benighted as not to have known these great folk. Albert and Frances brought to their papers names in the theater. The slightest question on our part would bring Albert to his feet, demonstrating the characteristics of that actor's performance, or reviving a scene, or a comedian's walk, mannerism, way of speech, in a performance so delightful we frequently prolonged our protests of ignorance in order to goad Albert to extend his imitation. The General's field, by way of her leadership in civil rights, civil liberties and women's organizations, was politics, government, music—and more. She knew the first names of Moussorgsky, Scriabin and the like, and we had no biographical dictionary by which to check her positiveness. Bob's musical knowledge was as wide as hers. To her discomfiture, he only put down names she had not thought of.

Charlton had a specialized field in addition to general knowledge. She had been elected a few months earlier the first woman president of the 125-year-old and many-branched Children's Aid Society in New York. In reaching that position, she has known and worked with branches of social service not only in New York but throughout the country. She drew from that wide area names for her list; the rest of us were ashamed to admit ignorance of these citizens. I did not need the game as a pointing finger at my lack of specialized knowledge. Mine could only be classified as heterogeneous.

Exhausted finally by argument and hilarity, we tapered off with a quick round of naming aloud cities with appropriate states starting with a given letter. The time limit was one minute. When Albert defiantly offered Lousy, New Jersey, the game was called off and we went to bed.

Chapter 7

The first remarkable sight on that Long Day's Journey was a loaf of bread. It looked like a dartboard; it was approximately the same size and was hung against the wall at the far end of the dining room side of the lounge. Coming up for breakfast, each one of us noticed it immediately, with varying comments of astonishment. Was it a kind of dartboard to supplant the telephone game? Could it be real? Where had it come from? It had come from the market Michel and the girls had visited the day before. They had not thought it extraordinary; they had seen many such; it was simply a variation of the customary tubular loaves. But Linda, helping in the kitchen to unpack the provisions, had protested she had never seen its like and was sure this was true for the rest of us. She had insisted on displaying it for our benefit. Afterward we said that somehow its incongruity had been like an official seal stamped on the day, to verify that it was special.

We had gone through locks before but we had not on this

trip or any preceding one counted twenty-four locks and three tunnels in one day. Actually we had not before been through any tunnel, and these were far from being just "any." Another specialty of the day was the rain that came and went, driving us indoors and bringing us out again on deck and on shore for such times as the intervals between showers coincided with the filling of a lock. Sam called our location the rain belt.

"All rain scenes should be shot here," he said. "Wouldn't have to wait more than a minute or two."

The final special quality of the day was the countryside.

We were on deck, the full company, because the sun was out, the view extraordinary. When Bob said, "I brought along quite a lot of reading, but I'm not even going to bring a book from my cabin any more." He turned to Sophy as he was talking. "You tried to tell me this is how it would be and it wasn't that I didn't believe you. I just couldn't picture it and I can't really take it in even now. Here we are moving at about three kilometers an hour, and I thought I'd look up from time to time to enjoy the countryside. I couldn't imagine how it constantly changes. A whole landscape shifts as we go round a bend, and Lord, the activity that goes on constantly, characters to talk to at the locks . . ."

Charlton at the moment coming in from the deck overheard him and joined in. "That's exactly what I'm trying to say. I'm writing to Stowe, and reading it over I see that I keep repeating the same thing over and over, how absolutely calm and tranquil and heavenly relaxing it is, but there's so much to do we never seem to have time to lie out on the deck the way he and I do when we're on sailing cruises.

"I don't want to sound smug," Sophy proffered, "but I can't help telling you both the rest of us have something over you." They looked their surprise.

Sophy nodded. "It's that the rest of us have done it

before, so we've got over being surprised. Now we have a double satisfaction in its being the way we remembered. But this is not like any landscape I saw on the other *Palinurus* trip. Nothing gentle about it."

On either side, steep cliffs barricaded the green fields we usually slipped between. At the top of these ravines we saw woods, so thick they almost blotted out the daylight.

Another shower caught us and we ducked inside to watch and marvel at the competence and strength of Sylvianne as we approached a lock. In a yellow slicker and hat and high boots, she ran back and forth, coiling, uncoiling, throwing and handling the great heavy, soggy ropes, as if they were beanbags for children.

A stout man on the drawbridge, arms folded across its railing, stolidly watched our approach. The current shower was a rain heavy enough to look like a falling curtain of steel knitting needles. Our observer wore not one article of rain protection—coat, hat or boots. He stood impassive, the water racing down his hair, his face, and soaking into his clothes. Richard called to him from the bridge.

"Vous avez l'air d'un canard." It was a simple statement telling the man he looked like a duck. Albert, watching the proceedings from just inside the door between deck and lounge, heard Richard's comment and misunderstood it, because Albert's grasp of French is not firm. He mistook the word *canard* for *canaille*. By the quixotic pattern all beginners in a foreign language follow, the words least likely to be called into use are the ones learned. Albert, it turned out, did not know that *canard* is French for "duck." What he *had* learned was that *canaille* is the word for "scoundrel, scum of the earth." Jerking open the doors, he flung himself on deck, the rest of us staring after him bewildered, except Frances, who leapt after him, asking in one breath what on earth he was doing and telling him for heaven's sake to come in at once. He was standing feet

apart, head back, hands cupped round his mouth, and he was shouting up at Richard in tones of urgency.

"For God's sake, Richard, this could mean war."

By the time the misunderstanding had been clarified, the situation did not make Albert's prophecy seem so exaggerated. Captain Richard's bellowed requests for the lock to be opened were met with the same impassivity by the duck on the drawbridge as our approach had been. Sylvianne, her hands raw and lobster red against her yellow slicker, was waiting poised with coiled rope, to toss it or jump ashore with it. Since no one came out of the lockkeeper's house and the watcher from the bridge neither moved nor spoke, Sylvianne, water- and impedimenta-logged as she was, jumped ashore with the coil of rope. Richard, coming down at full speed from the bridge, followed almost immediately after her and together they moored us. Without a glance or a word at the silent sentinel, Richard went into the lockkeeper's cottage.

We were all at windows watching this drama and Sam made a pronouncement. "That man over there"—pointing —"is an overseer. You can tell that because he doesn't lift a hand. That's the mark of a superintendent."

Richard came out of the house, fuming. He looked in on us briefly. "That's French logic. The lockkeeper is at lunch. Also there is a boat on the other side waiting to come through. When the lunch hour is over the so-and-so will return to business—and that boat's got the right of way. I can't tell from our side how large it is. I hope to God small enough to edge past us. If not"—with a shrug that created its own shower—"we'll have to back, and when I say back, I mean almost to our starting point today, where there's wide enough space to pass. That man"—nodding toward the bridge—"is a lock superintendent."

A woman came out of the house and went to the platform from which the gates were operated. She began at once to

wind round and round a great iron spoke like the crank of a very old automobile. The superintendent moved. At her approach he left the bridge, giving her full leeway without interference and certainly without a hand. He exchanged a friendly good-bye with the lady, waved at all of us, to our astonishment, and rode off on a bicycle—"to oversee the next lock," Sam said.

We left the arena in order to have lunch, but immediately after were back at our watching posts. We had gone through another lock, into a passage between steep cliffs, rocks jutting out over the surface with scraggly vegetation between, and still at the top on either side the same lowering woodland, and had come into the lock of Sardy.

It was exactly two forty-five, the General said, when a man on a bicycle hailed us from the towpath. We heard his halloos and came on deck. The rain had stopped, the sun was out, the deck was even showing dry patches. Our visitor looked earnestly from one of us to the next, probing each face and figure. Suddenly, and without the usual leisurely exchange of phrases that prefaces a French conversation, our investigator asked abruptly and urgently if we were Americans. At the instant of our corroboration he righted the bicycle lying beside him on the ground. No one of us, we realized, had seen him arrive. He pedaled off furiously as if he were in a race. He was back before we were ready to quit the lock, though we would have urged Richard to delay a little, because, we agreed, we had a feeling the man was coming back. Seeing him approach again, we left the boat and were waiting on the towpath when he arrived, too breathless to speak. Dismounting and flinging the bicycle on its side, he brought out from under his workman's blouse and handed to Bob, who was nearest, something covered in cellophane that looked like a small diploma.

Looking at it, Bob's eyes widened. Turning to the rest of us, he said a little shakily, "Well, I'll be damned! It's a

71

citation for this man from Eisenhower," and he read it aloud, translating as he read that this brave soldier was receiving a citation for acts of exceptional bravery. The document was signed: D. D. Eisenhower. When each of us had read—and we were all perceptibly moved as we handled it—we asked the man to tell us a little about the circumstances.

This area, he explained, had been a very important center in the Resistance movement. Bob interpolated, "It's just the terrain for it." English and American soldiers—the man pointed up and on either side—had been dropped here by parachute and dispatched on their separate missions. We shook hands all round, we congratulated him, we thanked him for showing us his treasure, we felt honored to have seen it and to have met him. He carefully put the document under his blouse again, raised and mounted his bicycle and rode off, half turning at the bend ahead to wave good-bye. We went inside. The rain was with us again.

Some time later Mildred spoke. "Did anyone get his name?" Only at that moment I realized there had been no conversation among us since the man had waved good-bye. We were all doubtless thinking of him and the place, what things he must have done to earn that citation, what people had come and gone in the night, because no one asked Mildred what man she was talking about.

"It was written on his citation," Charlton reminded us, "but I don't remember it." No one remembered it.

"Perhaps"—Frances seemed to be thinking aloud—"the whole thing had such a sort of unreality about it we didn't want to tack it down with facts. It's been like coming into a strange country by the look of it and suddenly out of nowhere a man appears. Where did he come from? How did he know the *Palinurus* was here? What made him think we might be Americans? He came, he let us touch a fragment of the history of this place, he made us see for a minute another time, a dark time, and he has gone."

The General stood up. "We won't ever forget this place; the unknown soldier put his stamp on it. I'm going on deck. The rain's stopped and we're out of the woods." Most of us trailed after her. Sam and Albert remained in the lounge, declaring they were going to read; they were exhausted by what Albert called "all this helter-skelter."

We were now out of one lock and into another in such rapid succession they seemed to be double, and with each one the banks rose higher and what we could see of the terrain on either side more thickly wooded than it had been at Sardy, so that though the sun was out we were in a kind of twilight. When we had counted six or seven locks—there was some argument about this—Bob pointed to a signboard on the current one and we read with some amusement the name Fussy. Charlton noted first the cornerstone in the lockkeeper's house, that read the lock had been built in 1826. There was argument among us whether by means of all these locks we had covered a distance of three, or four, miles. The day before we had gone through a lock named Petite Corvée. Even Bob had not known the meaning of the word *corvée* and looked it up, reporting gleefully the definition was "a bore," i.e., "drudgery." Mildred reminded us of this as we waited for the gates to open at Fussy. She would have transposed "Petite Corvée" to any of the locks we had just gone through. She was to say later she considered Fussy the most appropriate name in the whole series. Immediately beyond its gate we rounded a bend, the first deviation in the series. Charlton the sailor gave a long, low whistle.

"This is going to be tough going," she said, "to get such a long boat around an elbow turn like this. You see, he's heading for the bank in order to get the stern clear, then he'll have to swing the bow around again. Please God we don't get a cross wind." She might have been giving a stage

73

direction; a cross wind as we were nearing the bank drove us straight into it. We were grounded, with our bow stuck in bulrushes. Sam put his head out the door.

"Is it helter-skelter again?"

We answered him it was. Sophy had gone immediately to the bow to supervise the operation and to take pictures. Sam, on the run and calling out advice and encouragement, joined Sophy, bringing with him a spate of nautical terms, all wildly inaccurate but lavishly distributed. The lock-keeper, answering Richard's and Sylvianne's halloos, ran out from her lodge, to which she had returned after waving us off, gathered up a long pole on her way, raced across the narrow platform between the wheels that operate the lock, and waded in among the bulrushes. Leaning with all her strength against the end of the pole, she pushed our bow. Sylvianne, with a tremendous leap from the deck, joined and pushed with her. Michel, Fabienne and a girl I had never seen before came running along the catwalk. Passing us, they went to the tip of the bow. The stranger was young, slim, her tawny hair blowing into the wind. I called Mildred's attention to her.

"That must be Richard's girl. I don't know where he's been keeping her all this time."

Mildred said she wouldn't be surprised if somebody else popped up; and on the instant the black puppy barked directly over our heads. She had come from the captain's navigation post and ran back and forth the length of the roof. By this time we had something in the nature of an anvil chorus, Richard calling down to the lockkeeper with her pole, the lockkeeper answering, Sylvianne reporting the situation in a voice very like Ethel Merman's, Sam bellowing suggestions and encouragement, the puppy barking. Albert opened the doors from the lounge and looked out. "Is anything going on?"

Since I was the nearest, I was the only one who heard him.

"We're grounded," I bawled.

"My, my," was Albert's answer as he closed the doors.

Thanks to the workers at the pole and Richard's skillful maneuvering, we were afloat again; the shouting and the tumult died. Richard backed for another try from our starting point. Fabienne swung the boom toward shore and Sylvianne, jumping up to catch it, pushed off from the bank and came on board. She sent the boom across to the lockkeeper, who followed the same technique. The lockkeeper called up to Richard that she would stay with us in case further assistance was needed. Linda, at Richard's and the lockkeeper's suggestion, went ashore, borrowed the lockkeeper's bicycle and rode off to give the news at the next lock and ask the keeper there to be on the alert in case any further mishap occurred. The girls in the stern went back inside with Michel, the puppy rejoined Richard, and after a few minutes of talk and speculation over what had happened, the rest of us moved inside, to find Albert sound asleep, a book outspread on his lap. He roused at once and welcomed us cordially.

"You know, Albert," Sam told him, "the way you go to sleep over a book and drop it over and over, you turn it from hard-cover to paperback."

Albert admitted this. "Maybe I should read standing up."

Bob, joining in, said wistfully he wished he could go to sleep as easily as Albert seemed to. Once there, he went through the night without a break, but the drifting off seemed endless and he did not like to take sleeping pills. Sam immediately offered a solution. When Bob was in bed, Sam would bring him Albert's book. According to Albert's standard, this would require only a very few minutes for Bob, then Sam would tiptoe in, retrieve it and return it to

Albert for his own dropping off.

While we waited at the next lock, Bob read its name, Mondain, with the comment that he could do with its being more mundane than Fussy had been. We had all come on deck again, but were paying very little attention to Bob because we were transfixed at the sight of one of Linda's two companions. One of these was obviously the lock-keeper, since he was already at the wheel, a surprise in itself because this was a man. But our greater astonishment was at the sight of Linda's other companion, the old bridge-watcher from way back, the supervisor, and he was holding a long pole. Mildred wondered if he'd been doing a little fishing to help pass the time, but when he actually lowered the pole into the water and began industriously removing bits of water vegetation we had accumulated around and on our bow in our grounding and the narrow channel, Frances said we had been unjust, he had been waiting for an opportunity to work as well as oversee. As soon as we were through he put down the pole and rushed off ahead of us, calling out he would be waiting at the next lock.

"First he was a mute and now he's a regular blabber-mouth," was Sam's comment.

Linda relinquished the bicycle to the Fussy lockkeeper and came on board. Madame Fussy rode back to her post, Richard calling down his good-byes and renewed thanks. Sam and Albert went back to read, they said, Sam interjecting, "That's at least what Albert calls it." Mildred followed them with the determination, she said, to work on her needlepoint at least ten minutes without interruption. Michel came from the catwalk to the forward deck so quietly I had not noticed him until with a shy, scarcely audible *"Pardon, madame,"* he indicated he would like to move where I was standing. I was interfering with the approach to his herb garden, what had seemed to us a nondescript assortment of flats across and on top of the forward hatch. I asked if

76

he came here often. We had not seen him before, at least I had not and the others corroborated. He seemed mildly surprised, but yes, he told us, he came every day, twice a day, to select fresh herbs for lunch and for dinner.

"Well," Charlton said when he had left, "I knew he was shy—he looks about to run if you speak to him—but I didn't realize he was invisible. Can you believe Sylvianne is his wife?"

We looked again at Sylvianne standing in the bow. She had taken off her slicker and rain hat; she was wearing slacks and a red sweater and she had pushed up the sleeves though we were shivering in sweaters and coats. It was late afternoon, overcast; the air was damp and raw. Sylvianne's arms and hands were red, but Sophy said, "Look at their strength and competence." Sylvianne was standing, feet wide apart, ready with a coil of rope and calling up to Richard a number and then another number.

"I've heard her do that many times," Bob said, "and I meant to ask her what it meant, but she's always been so busy I didn't dare."

We were into the lock, the ropes had been thrown and secured, Richard joined us unexpectedly. He had come down, he said, for a bit of a stretch to get ready for the tunnels ahead. He admitted he was a little fagged; this was the roughest day of the cruise. From tomorrow on it would all be easy and smooth, but before we tied up at Baye there would be a few more locks, three tunnels, and then we would be in port. Bob said, now that he had the chance, he wanted to ask what it was Sylvianne called up each time we came into a lock.

"Numbers," Richard told him. "The number of inches between my boat and the side of the canal. From the bow, being on the level, she can see them much better than I can up there. I have the sense of it, but I like to have it checked and verified. Sylvianne's never done this kind of work before, you know," he added, "and by Jove she's learned fast. I never have any doubt about the inches she's calling. I leave it to her, her eye is so accurate." Out of the lock now, he was crouched, making ready to jump ashore, and turned back to add, "That's how narrow these channels are—an inch off and we're in trouble." He jumped.

"And that's supernavigating," Charlton called after him.

We all stood on deck for the experience of going through the first tunnel. Bob showed us on the chart this one was called Souterre-des-Breulles, *souterre* being the word for "tunnel." He explained on the canal chart that had become his bible, *souterre* was abbreviated to *sout*. From this fountainhead he also brought the information that this tunnel would be 212 meters, the next one 268 and the final one 758. The General pointed out since all of us with the exception of the Jaffes lived in New York, and for the Jaffes New York was a second home, she did not anticipate any supernatural quality in our passage underwater. They would be smaller and simpler versions of the Holland and Lincoln. When we emerged from Souterre-des-Breulles she was the first to acknowledge her misapprehension.

"I take it all back," she said. "This was really eerie. Two hundred and twelve meters in total blackness is not like the Holland Tunnel."

"I think it's the silence too," Bob said, and he was almost whispering, "and the aloneness."

"Of course there's no cross wind or any wind," Charlton offered, "but how does Richard keep on center? By osmosis? *That's* eerie."

Someone suggested we go inside to wait for the next tunnel and no one demurred. The moment we were in lights and warmth there was lively conversation. We came out again at the approach to the second tunnel. It was getting colder with every meter, was Sam's opinion. Bob's rejoinder was to thank God and Sam for the loan of Sam's jacket. We admitted afterward each of us had thought to be an old tunnel hand by the time we reached the second and had expected to ride through the passage with nonchalance, but throughout its length no one made jokes, no one even spoke. We could hear the water lapping against the side of the channel and somewhere water dripping; there was no sound from our engines.

When we came inside to wait for the third and last tunnel, Linda met us. Richard had sent word if it was convenient for us, he would appreciate our leaving the lounge so that the lights could all be put out and not be distracting through the long passage; and would we in our cabins draw the curtains?

This seemed a good time to change for dinner. We went below, reminding one another on the stairs and in the corridor not to forget to draw the curtains. Before I turned on the light in my cabin I looked through the window. I do not remember ever seeing such total thick blackness.

Albert's voice came sharply into the corridor.

"Did anybody see Frances leave the deck? She's not in her cabin." Every door opened, everyone protesting ignorance of her whereabouts. Albert was already halfway up the stairs. "My God, I think she's still out there," he called back. We heard him fumbling at the doors. Sam and Bob had started after him, but the General called out she thought we had all better stay where we were.

"We'll just muddle things up groping around in the dark." We recognized the logic of this and fell back. We all crowded around the foot of the stairs. It seemed time beyond counting until we heard the doors open again and Albert's voice.

"I've got her. She's O.K." They came down the stairs into the light of the corridor, Albert wide-eyed and perceptibly shaken. Frances was shaking too, with cold and rage.

"I'm frozen but I was having the most wonderful experience of my life, and you made me leave it."

"You couldn't have found your way to the doors. Groping around, you could have hurt yourself or something."

"I wouldn't have been groping because I didn't want to come inside, and where could I have gone? You could hardly think I could go overboard in this channel. I am frozen," she conceded, and her teeth were chattering.

When I came upstairs for dinner we were still in the tunnel, but as I looked through the closed doors I could see light ahead. We were approaching the far end. Charlton came up behind me, and involuntarily we opened the doors and stepped out, cold as it was. I think we wanted to be on hand at the end of this journey. We were not talking, but watching the opening ahead grow larger and the blackness changing to gray. Simultaneously we saw birds, we thought, in flight back and forth across the grayness. Birds?

"Bats," we told each other, and our voices were almost as high above the human scale as a bat's squeak. As we communicated this to each other, we turned as one person for the door and as one person were wedged in it.

There was no nonsense of "Go ahead," or "After you." Neither could go ahead or after the other. We were unhappily synchronized. Telling each other to be calm, breathe in, pull in our stomachs, wriggle our shoulders, we popped out of the doorway and into the lounge, slammed the doors behind us. The others were coming up the stairs. Fabienne was setting the table.

"The captain wishes me to say," she told us in French, "we are at Baye and Michel asks that he may serve dinner in an hour."

"It's exactly seven forty-five," the General said, "and the ice is here."

Chapter 8

It is disconcerting to a passenger when a barge becomes one of the things that go bump in the night. A barge at the end of the day is securely tied fore and aft. Sylvianne did this for us, winding heavy ropes around iron stakes. Richard drove these in on the bank, one at the bow and one at the stern. He used a formidable iron mallet, the kind that used to strike a gong to announce the opening of an Arthur Rank motion picture. Even Sylvianne could not wield ours; I had seen her try once. Our *Palinurus* would then snuggle alongside the bank and not stir until she was unleashed the next morning.

She did not behave at Baye in such a docile, submissive manner. Frequently during the night I was wakened by her restlessness, bumping, scraping and groaning. There was a high wind, I could hear that. I had heard winds on other nights, and rain, but neither of these elements had disturbed our equilibrium.

Ruminating over this as I dressed in the morning, I allowed the night to have had dramatic justice; it had not been enough for us to go through the crises of the long day. To come to a complete stop with our arrival at Baye would have been too abrupt; we had to taper off into our customary placidity.

The drama, at least the dramatic contrast, was not yet finished. I came up the stairs to the lounge for breakfast, and what to my wondering eyes should appear but a lake and a stone quay. We had not been attached by spikes to a bank; we were moored at a quay and in a channel wide enough to give the *Palinurus* leeway for bumping and scraping and backing and butting. In the guidebook the lake at Baye is called an *étang* and in the dictionary an *étang* is a pond, but in the opinion of one who had been traveling along a channel whose margin on either side of the vessel was measured in inches, the body of water at Baye is a lake.

No one was on deck to share my astonishment, but the sun was out, the air was clear and crisp, the smell of autumn in it, so I went ashore. Beyond a little grove of trees I reached a bridge, and crossing it, walked along a dirt road bordered on one side by a canal, not the one on which we had been traveling, and on the other by a row of small houses, each set back from a charming garden neatly laid out in precise rows of flowers, mostly dahlias, alternating with mouth-watering vegetables; overhanging each garden a pear tree, the pears hanging so heavily they must have been almost ripe for picking. I had retraced my path and was halfway across the grove of trees when I saw Sophy coming toward me. I said I would go back with her because I wanted to show her the road and the gardens I had found, but especially to relish with her a particular sign I had read. She stipulated we wait a minute or two to see something she thought we would both enjoy.

"I've given Richard the keys to the Volkswagen," she said. "He's going back to get it and he's taking Michel to do some marketing. I want to see them leave."

We both with joy saw them leave a few minutes later on a diminutive motorcycle—a *Mobilette,* I found out later. Richard was in the driver's seat; Michel was behind him, on a seat, I suppose, but his feet were extended rigidly on either side, and even while we watched, twice one foot either by inadvertence or exhaustion touched the ground, causing Richard to exercise serpentine convolutions and threatening to dislodge them both.

Sophy was as satisfactorily pleased as I had been at the sign I had discovered along the road by the other canal. Our pleasure was only in its absurdity when translated literally, and that is a pastime we both enjoy. In literal English it read: "Fishing is prohibited here even with a delicate line floating from the hand."

The full company, except Mildred, had assembled for breakfast in scattered formation at separate tables when Sophy and I returned. Sam was just returning up the stairs after attending Mildred with coffee in her cabin. Bob and Albert were bewildered by our exchanges about the disturbance of our sleep during the night because of bumps and groans and creaks. Bob said he did not remember ever having gone to sleep so promptly and slept so uninterruptedly.

"You see," Sam told us, "that's from giving him Albert's book to read. Albert was already unconscious when I took it away from him."

We were still at the table when I heard and recognized the silly popping sounds of the *Mobilette* engine, like a series of agitated expostulations. With almost the same agitated expostulations I coaxed, herded and drove my companions to the deck to watch the arrival of its passengers, an enjoyable sight the audience acknowledged with cheers. We saw Michel's stiffly extended feet and legs and nothing more of him until Richard, dismounting, unveiled the upper part of his passenger, curtained behind loaves of bread.

With some asperity and anxiety, the General wanted to know if they had been unable to find the Volkswagen. Richard reassured her; he was helping Michel to stand, bend his knees and walk, but he paused to give her reassurance.

"No trouble at all. We drove it ahead and parked it just beyond the Bazolles locks—that's our next stop. We left the other provisions locked inside, took out our trusty little *Mobilette,* came on her, and here we are." He resumed flexing Michel's knees.

Sophy turned back to us. "Do you realize," she asked, "on that ridiculous little machine in the space of less than an hour they have covered and gone beyond the mileage of our whole day—and what a day—yesterday?"

"But, Sophy, darling," was Frances's comment, "we'd have missed the tunnels."

We stayed on deck to savor the new experience of descending locks. Richard had told us Baye would be our peak of ascent. "It's not far from Baye to the lock of Bazolles and for the first time we enter on the high side and are lowered to meet the grade beyond." As we were being lowered—the sensation was not unlike going down in an elevator—Sophy declared that psychologically she felt we had come to the top of the world.

Corbigny, the guidebook says, is a little city situated at the *confins* of the Morvan and of the Nivernais and known for its *foires.* Wanting to make sure that *foires* meant "fairs," I looked the word up in the dictionary. To my surprise, I found it not only means "fairs," but also is the French for "diarrhea." I know there are many double meanings in the English language, but at the moment I could not think of any so widely apart.

We drove to Corbigny, the General at the wheel. Richard had told her, she reported, he would bring the barge on to Mont-et-Marre, moor, and wait for us. There was no fair that day, but at the post office we had our own. As usual, leaving the car, we had scattered. My first errand was to buy stamps. I was not surprised to find Frances and Albert with postcards on the same errand; only that they had found their way ahead of me. They had not asked directions.

"Frances has a nose for post offices," Albert explained.

Sam and Mildred came in soon after for airmail stamps to America.

The attendants were a young girl and an elderly woman, spare, gray-haired, thin-lipped and, behind her pince-nez, sharp-eyed. I was asked by its members to be spokesman for our group.

At my request the young girl looked dismayed, almost frightened. She turned questioningly to her companion, whose lips at the request had tightened even more narrowly, and she did not speak. The young girl, feeling herself, I think, cast adrift, turned back to me. This would not be possible, she said, and to my inquiry if they were out of stamps, the girl shook her head vigorously: Oh, no, not at all, she insisted, they had many, many stamps.

"In that case"—I am afraid my voice was ominously patient—"would it be possible for me to have some of those stamps for my mail?"

Replying to this, the young clerk raised her voice almost to a shout, a characteristic of people who feel if they speak their own language loud enough the other person must of course understand; obviously her customer's obtuseness was due to unfamiliarity with the language. The voice rang through the post office, gathering to the counter a group of interested bystanders, who had come in on their own errands. This tended to accelerate my loss of patience. I spoke slowly, quietly, each syllable a deadly thrust, I hoped, at the agitated clerk. The older woman, bringing up the heavy artillery, closed ranks with the girl and opened fire.

"Because, madame," she pronounced with awesome dignity, "with a stamp affixed to a postcard or a letter the cost would be greater due to the added weight of the stamp. Look, I will show you. Give me a letter, please." She took one from the handful that in a kind of hypnosis I extended toward her. "Thank you, madame."

Within her arm's reach there was a small scale on the counter. She drew this toward her and placed the letter on it. Leaning back a little, she opened a drawer immediately in front of her, withdrew what looked like the sort of copybook children use at school, riffled through its pages, revealing sheets of stamps of varying denominations. She selected one of these, took from it a single stamp, and like a conjuror showing what he will make disappear, she waved it at all of us.

"Now, if you will observe closely." She placed the stamp on the center of the letter on the scale, withdrew her hand delicately and spoke to me with tolerance.

"Now I have shown you that a stamp affixed adds to the weight; therefore the cost would be greater. But it is impossible to estimate how much greater; therefore you see we cannot sell you a stamp."

This logic baffled me and, translated, baffled my companions. In the face of such difficulty, that certainly one could not fail to recognize, we had no alternative to suggest. The girl relaxed at once, smiling eagerly; even Minerva at the scales nodded.

However, the young one offered, they had now in this post office the very latest invention, a machine for the stamping. If we would give her whatever was to be mailed it would be put instantly through the machine, which knew what was required. It was the affixing of a stamp, one must understand, that was impossible.

Sam had been edging closer and closer to the scene of action until at the moment of weighing he was leaning over the counter, his head nearly touching the scales. I think, like the girl, who shouted in order to make the language understood, he reasoned the nearer to the speaker he placed himself, the greater the possibility of his understanding and translating the language. This method had not been successful; a more direct approach was required.

"What the hell is all this?" He put it simply. I translated for his benefit and Mildred's, and catching sight of Frances's and Albert's obvious bewilderment, raised my voice to include them and also to drown out the babel among the bystanders. They were assuring one another of the logic and the excellence of this postal mechanism and the unfortunate lack of understanding on the part of the foreigners. Were they English, they inquired of one another, or American? Without the ability to deal immediately and effectively with a critical situation, Sam would not have reached the top position in the motion picture world that he had occupied for many years. He dealt with this one.

"Tell her," he instructed, "now that we understand, in future we will buy our postcards, bring them and our letter paper in envelopes to her to put through the machine. Then we will take them home, write our messages and drop them ourselves in a letter box."

Assuring Sam of the excellence of this idea, I communicated it to the two custodians. The response was an emphatic negative; the young woman was its spokesman. This would not do at all, she told us. Everything must be brought to the post office, relinquished, put through the stamping machine and mailed immediately. It was a rule that the stamping and the mailing should be simultaneous. We would then be told how much we owed, but we could not buy stamps. I translated this ultimatum concisely.

"No stamps. It's all done by machine. What they showed us for demonstration was a leftover, I suppose."

When we left the building, we had relinquished our mail, paid the amounts required, shaken hands with the two attendants and some of the bystanders, settling their speculations by telling them we were Americans.

Sam looked at his watch. "It has taken forty-five minutes," he told us, "to learn that Corbigny has a stamping machine."

Frances was not reconciled, she said. She did not mind the time spent but she bemoaned the absence of stamps, because French stamps were so pretty, it had been a pleasure to put them on.

Within a block of the post office we were scattered again. Walking alone, I saw something I thought a little tempting in a shop and turned back to tell the others. There was no one of our group in sight. Resuming my own ambling, I came abreast of Sophy and Charlton looking in a window. A little farther on we met Bob. He told us he needed to send a cable; did we happen to know where the post office was? I did happen, I told him, and he was in for quite a happening. I wished him strength and fortitude and sent him on his way.

Sophy was looking for a camera shop, she said. Her camera had become increasingly unsatisfactory; she was afraid she would have to buy a new one and might better do it now than risk bad pictures. I endorsed this heartily; the General includes in her offices taking the pictures on each trip, later assembling them and making an album for each traveler, a souvenir as appealing to us as postcards to the Hacketts. Albert is an eager photographer too, but not so dependable, owing to a tendency on his part to forget to put film in his camera.

Separating once more, I wandered on to the end of the street and came back on the opposite side, looking in each window but finding nothing tempting until I saw the General and her daughter in a camera shop. The moment of my arrival was heaven-sent for my enjoyment. The General had just purchased an Instamatic; the saleswoman, young, brisk, efficient, was explaining in a spate of technical vocabulary its construction and operation.

From the glazed look in her eye and the portentous nod of her head, it was obvious the General for all her declarations of proficiency was out of her depth in this French. Charlton caught my eye and moved to the doorway to share my enjoyment. When we heard our linguist thank the saleslady with the assertion that now everything was understood perfectly, Charlton and I moved hastily to the sidewalk and were decently composed when Sophy joined us. There was no mention made of the transaction other than congratulations at finding in the town an adequate camera shop and a replacement.

Still together, we visited a *boulangerie*. Sophy wanted, she said, to buy some candy because our store on the boat was rapidly diminishing and the others would not want to be without it. Charlton and I voiced some skepticism at such altruism and Sophy, admitting shamefacedly her devious approach, moved to a counter, Charlton and I just behind her. The proprietress coming forward to serve Sophy looked beyond her at us with an expression of mounting indignation and disfavor. For the moment I could not imagine why Charlton and I had incurred this, and then I realized we were both sniffing the air like beagles. The proprietress, misinterpreting this, thought we had encountered a bad smell. To emphasize our reassurance that ours were sniffs of appreciation, we bought such an assortment of pastries we were too encumbered when we left to do any further shopping and headed for the car.

On our way we talked about the *boulangerie,* its importance in the town. No matter how small the place, there would always be bakeries, each one boasting beautiful pastries as well as breads and buns. This was a kind of sophistication that would prevail in every community, and certainly each would contain more than one bakeshop. Unlike Ireland, Sophy reminded me, harking back to an earlier trip, where the ratio was five pubs to a block.

Bob was already at the car when we reached it, arrived there, he said, only a few minutes earlier, and the whole intervening time spent at the post office. He had enjoyed —a questionable term—the services of the two women who had ministered to us. They had been unable to estimate the cost of the cable he wished to send because, they admitted after a lengthy conference in the far corner to which they had retreated, they did not know how to count the words, that is, whether the name and address should be included in the overall count. Bob had assured them he had sent many cables from many places and the standard procedure was the same everywhere, and he explained it. They were politely skeptical. In Corbigny, they told him, it could very well be different. They had retired again to their conference corner.

The older woman reported the sense of that meeting. "It is necessary that we speak to the director." To carry out this decision, Bob said, obviously required boldness. It was with a visible squaring of the shoulders that the two marched across the back of the room and disappeared. They returned presently with a dapper, brisk, stocky gentleman. He was shorter than either of the two women but by Bob's guess a contemporary of the older one—in spite of contradictory efforts by way of hair blacker than nature produced, swirled gracefully over unmistakable baldness and ending along one side in a curled fringe. He wore, Bob reported, over a rather shiny blue suit, detachable sleeve protectors and carried, hooked over one outspread thumb, a pair of nose glasses. In his other hand he held the telegraph blank that contained Bob's message, and putting it on the counter, extended it to Bob, at the same time jabbing at the message with an ink-stained finger.

" 'Now you see, monsieur, certainly I shall give you the

cost of this message. It is of the greatest simplicity'—accompanying this with a ferocious scowl of disapproval upward at the two women."

Bob was now acting the scene, and we were spellbound. " 'However, I will show an error, very grave, on the part of monsieur.' He pushed the cable form at me, at the same time wagging fiercely in front of my face the thumb with the glasses on it. I'm afraid I jumped back, in fact, I know I did, because he soothed me. 'It is an error that can, happily, be corrected, do you see? It is permitted by the rules to make a message of twenty-two words.' He breathed deeply, with a sucking noise. 'But you, monsieur, you have employed only nineteen. Surely there is something more that you can add.' "

The country we drove over to Corbigny, and from there to Mont-et-Marre, was as different from the wild, sinister landscape we had gone through the day before as if they were several hundred miles apart. It was almost impossible to realize, Sophy said, the distance between them was less than twenty. Now we were passing through wide landscapes of cultivated fields, of hills rimming the distance almost all the way around, with lightly wooded areas punctuating the fields. Mildred asked us to realize how beautiful French woodlands always were and how unlike any others, because here the underbrush was all cleared away and usually the woods themselves thinned, allowing light to filter through, bringing a constantly changing color. In an undertone to me she added, "And no châteaux for Sam to buy and live in."

Between that fervent comment and Charlton's announcement I could not have counted ten.

"Look over there. Albert and I think this is one of the most beautiful châteaux we've seen on the trip. We found it on our bicycle tour, that night before the long day."

"It's a judgment on you," I said to Mildred. "You shouldn't have said the word aloud." Mildred shook her head; she was smiling and serene.

"Not today," she said, "not to worry today. Sam doesn't do or even talk business today."

Sam stayed in the car with Mildred; he did not even get out with the rest of us to look through tall, glorious wrought-iron gates half open to an inner walled courtyard carpeted with a lawn of such perfection it had the texture of cloth. Half-open wrought-iron gates again, at the far end of the courtyard, matching the entrance portal, gave onto the vine-covered façade of a château.

"Well," was Bob's comment, "there's nothing to say. I'm just sighing with utter contentment."

Back in the car, Charlton told us there was one other thing she and Albert would like us to see on the way back.

"If that's all right with you, Sam, and we're not taking too much time." Sam told her to go ahead; another half hour would be all right.

"It's a place where rabbits are kept," Charlton explained. "It's unusual and very pretty."

The chorus that broke out at this announcement was like a hailstorm. Jeers, expostulations: "Rabbits?" "It sounds just darling." "Pretty?" "After that glorious château?"

"All right," was Albert's answer. "You jeered before. Now look."

We had the grace to apologize. We were looking at a lawn that covered I should think at least an acre and was almost as beautifully kept as the one in the courtyard of the château. It was enclosed by a low wall of terra-cotta tile, and it was occupied by perhaps a hundred rabbits, most of them white, a lesser number beige. They were totally unconfined, their movement over the bright green made pictures unlike anything any of us had ever seen.

Immediately we reached the barge, Sam, waving to us,

92

said, "I'll see you at half-past six," and went below.

The preceding evening when we had gathered for drinks before dinner, Sam, coming from his cabin, had stopped at the head of the stairs.

"I told Mildred I'd like to tell you myself why I'm not going to join you tonight. I shall be giving observance to Yom Kippur. It's a time of prayer. I have my shawl, that's called a tallith, my yarmulke, that's my head covering, and my book of prayers."

With a grin he had added, *"Bon appetit.* How's that for French?" waved to us, turned, and was gone down the stairs again.

Mildred, joining us, had explained she herself did not keep these observances, it was not part of her form of belief, though she deeply respected Sam's, and, she added, it would make Sam very unhappy if we allowed his absence to affect whatever we wanted to do after dinner.

Almost before she had finished Bob had said with engaging shyness, as a matter of fact he had been asked to go with Richard and Richard's girl to a nearby café after dinner. He had hesitated to accept, though it sounded rather fun, because he hadn't wanted to seem a deserter of the group, but since Sam—and he smiled a little apologetically—had made a rift in the solid formation for quite a different reason, he too would desert for an evening.

Sophy and I had been vehement in our protests, talking over and across each other.

Sophy had repeated an expression she calls upon frequently: "It's a *nightmare* if anyone feels tied to the others; that's the very thing that makes this different from those guided and group tours where people are herded together."

Reassured, Bob had asked if Charlton would go with him, but she said she must catch up on letters and, if she got through them, would settle down cozily with her needlepoint and early bed. The Hacketts, Sophy and I had played Scrabble. Later, going down to bed, I had followed Sophy, and pointing to Sam's door as we passed it, said when we had reached our rooms how strange to see it closed, reminding her, and she nodded, he always stood on the threshold calling good-night messages to everyone that usually included names he had just thought of for the telephone game.

When we had come back from Corbigny at half-past four, Sam immediately excused himself. The pattern of observance, he told us, granted two hours' respite during the twenty-four. Now he would resume his prayers.

"That's why he would not talk about buying a château today?" I asked.

"Of course," was Mildred's answer.

At our usual time we were in the lounge having drinks. Mildred looked at her watch, put down her glass, took an orange from a bowl of fruit on the coffee table in front of her.

"I'll be back with Sam in a few minutes. I always share the final prayer with him and break his fast." When she had gone we turned involuntarily to one another, acknowledging what a moving experience for us this had been. Sam had observed his holy day without ostentation, no sense of imposing any ritual on the rest of us, but simply a quiet and dignified observance of tradition. We all felt a benefit and benediction from it.

Chapter 9

Albert was missing. The word went around at breakfast. He probably wanted a nice quiet place to read, Sam proferred, so if we visited the unoccupied cabins in the stern we would find him comfortably asleep.

We did not find him in any one of them, and since the barge was not of a size nor complicated architecture to provide out-of-the-way places, we had to realize he was not aboard. By the same reasoning, to have fallen overboard seemed unlikely. For that matter, Charlton pointed out, so did a solitary excursion, since it was raining. In her incisive estimate of a situation she is very like her mother.

However, in her very denial of a solitary excursion under such conditions she had given us a clue. It had not been raining earlier, I pointed out; I had wakened and dressed in sunlight. The rain had begun as I went on deck for a general look around and possible short walk. We had to believe Albert had done the same thing, only he had not come back. We put the matter to Richard. Better to go on, was his decision, than await his return. Either he would be waiting at the next lock or we would ease into the bank and return him to us somehow from the towpath.

The prospect of this was pleasing to everyone but Frances. She was not happy at our gleeful speculations about retrieving the wanderer by way of some kind of lasso or the boom. Frances, Sophy and I remembered that on the earlier *Palinurus* trip Albert, carried away by Richard's agility on the boom, had imitated it. He had not pushed hard enough from the bank and had come to a full stop over the water. Roused to superhuman effort by Frances's anguished commands not to fall in, he had somehow wriggled the pole into motion again and come within Richard's grasp, to be pulled ignominiously on deck and detached from his paralyzed grip on the pole.

"And *that*," Frances said, knowing what we were remembering, "was a few years ago."

We left off all further speculation and tried to reassure her his rescue this time would be less spectacular.

The rescue was not spectacular, nor was the sight of Albert. We found him at the lock, the rain cascading down his length almost visibly in ripples because he was shaking with cold. Before he disappeared again for a hot bath and change of clothes, he managed to tell us the morning had been so fine he had gone for a walk and enjoying it had gone so far it seemed foolish to come back, better to continue to the next lock, and then the rains had come. He had left the barge, he thought, around half-past seven. It was nine o'clock when we had taken off, the General said.

By lunchtime Albert seemed thoroughly restored and declared himself, wistfully, very hungry. Frances had asked for hot water and had made him several cups of Sanka. She had not asked for food, she told him, because it would be so inconsiderate to the girls, since breakfast was long over. Gentle aromas were drifting our way, tantalizing enough,

Bob said, to drive the rest of us to madness; he dared not even imagine Albert's emotional state. Bob was right, because the sight of the luncheon presented to us drew from Albert an expression that for him is coincidental with deep emotion.

"My, oh my, my," he said.

The main dish presented to us that day was worthy of Albert's expression of fervor. We had *moules,* cooked, by concession to the Hacketts' and my idiosyncrasy, without garlic. If anyone should challenge the possibility of making a succulent dish of *moules* without garlic, any one of us would pick up the gauntlet. Michel had done them with white wine, butter and herbs from his little bunch of flats. Even Sam and Mildred, who had admitted when they were at home the sun did not set for them on a day devoid of garlic, pronounced it a masterpiece.

Understandably we did not hurry immediately after lunch to further activity, but when we were a little less somnolent than at the conclusion of the meal we went ashore at Châtillon-en-Bazois, where we had docked just before lunch. We scattered as usual. Later, not unexpectedly, we found one another at the post office. Charlton and the Hacketts were already there when I arrived. Charlton at sight of me was cross, she said, because I had not been with her to enjoy the transaction she had just completed, as she had missed ours at Corbigny. She had arrived with a number of letters of varying weight and some postcards. Each one had been meticulously weighed more than once, with great deliberation and a number of conferences between the young woman who was taking care of her and the great panjandrum himself, unavailable to common folk. When the whole elaborate transaction had been finished—Charlton was savoring the climax—her batch had been tossed to join others that three-quarters filled an open baby-blue plastic latticework laundry basket.

97

"It has just been carried out," she said. "Evidently this is the way mail is transported. What price our sealed and padlocked mailbags at home?"

Albert and Frances had apparently come in after Charlton, and were waiting for her business to be concluded. Charlton left to do a little exploring, she said, but I moved over with the Hacketts in the hope their encounter with the postal service would be rewarding, and it was. The representative behind the counter of the postal service expressed her pleasure at seeing the postcards, explaining how agreeable it was not to have variations in weight, requiring, we must understand, very difficult estimation of cost. When we turned to go she detained us with a somewhat beseeching gesture. She would like to make a suggestion—from the tone of her voice it was more like an entreaty—that we refrain from writing letters but turn instead to the wonderful thing the post office could offer us, the aerogramme. When I had translated this, Frances nodded decisively.

"Then we must take some, Albert," she said. "She seemed so eager I think she would be hurt if we refused them."

"Not for me," I said, with equal firmness. "I'm never sure which side to write on; I invariably fold them the wrong way so the writing is outside. I want none of them."

That young woman is a loss to the Fuller Brush Company. Sensing in me a recalcitrant customer, she swung into an eloquent and dramatic appeal. What a convenience they were, already stamped and ready for the mailing, and of such a convenient size, not burdening one with the obligation to write a long letter but of exquisite proportion for one's needs. I yielded, if only to save Frances distress, and the supersaleswoman was highly gratified. We must wait, she told us, only a very small minute; she must go into the back room to secure them; there were none available on her counter.

Returning on a mincing run, she was already counting off the number she hoped we would take, but when she had spread her collection on the counter she looked up from her merchandise with an expression of such dismay Albert asked anxiously, "Do you think this has all been too much for her?"

She spoke and her voice trembled. "Now, as you will see, this is a little disaster. The supply, and it is all that we have at this moment, is not of the latest issue, and therefore it does not include the proper tariff. It is necessary that I obtain from the postmaster actual stamps."

She left us again and presently returned behind the postmaster, a tall man whose step was the tread of authority. He carried what was now a familiar sight, a copybook precisely like the one the postmaster at Corbigny had flourished. Placing it on the counter and riffling the pages, he extracted a number of stamps and handed them individually to his attendant. Moistening delicately with her tongue each offering from him, she affixed under his direction two to each aerogramme. The postmaster had not spoken to us, and with only a formal bow and a murmured "Mesdames, monsieur," he about-faced and made his measured exit. With considerable finger-counting, our now chastened saleslady totaled the amount we must pay. When this negotiation was done, complicated in itself because of change that had to be made, she had thought of a compensation and shared with us the silver lining.

"Now you have the extra stamp to take care of the weight of the stamps themselves, so you see what a convenience this is."

Frances was delighted, in fact a little smug.

"I've got stamps after all," she triumphed, "and aren't they pretty?"

The road away from the village looked inviting, so we followed it, still together. We passed a crossroads from the canal bridge, rounded a slight bend and a few yards farther stopped as simultaneously as if someone had called "Halt!" On our right we were looking through gates up a magnificent drive to a glorious château. The character of the village had given us no sense of such grandeur in its vicinity, and I protested to the others, when I could get my breath, there was no mention of it in the guidebook because I had looked to see what we might expect to find. The gates were ajar; we ventured to walk through them and up the driveway a short distance, but we turned back, seeing cars at the far end; obviously this great place was occupied and its owners in residence at the moment. We hurriedly retraced our steps and just beyond the gates saw Sam and Mildred strolling toward us. Albert called to him, "This is worth your considering, Sam."

"God help us," was Mildred's comment, adding firmly and half to herself, "Not to worry, not to worry."

Sam had moved ahead and now turned back to her.

"It's worth considering, Mildred," he said, "and it's good to have several prospects, because sometimes, you know, a deal can fall through."

Mildred cheered perceptibly. "That's a good idea," she encouraged him. "Get a number on the string. That could save me from any of them."

Sam ignored this. He was standing in deep concentration, feet apart, hands clasped behind his back. When he rejoined us he was shaking his head.

"Afraid this one won't do for you, Mildred. I think it would be too much for you to handle."

For our return we chose the opposite side of the road, and somehow we seemed all to be together again. To everyone's astonishment, we discovered over the wall edging the road and at a very considerable drop below it, we could look down on an acreage of vegetable gardens laid out as exactly as if they were squares on a gigantic checkerboard. Bob had been the first to discover them because he is considerably taller than any other member of our company. He had been able to look across the top of the wall —it was certainly two feet in breadth—and down to the scene below. His summons of "Hey, look what's down here" had brought the rest of us to uncomfortable positions of stretching and scraping our fronts across the wall top, but the sight below rewarded our discomfort. No one was working in any of the plots so, to our frustration, there was no one to ask about ownership. Our speculation was that they were part of the château property, a surmise disquieting to Sam.

"Perhaps we ought to reconsider, Mildred. You could oversee the work and I'd take on the marketing of what produce we didn't use. It might be quite a big thing, you know."

Serenity was in Mildred's smile when she caught my eye and, shaking her head, murmured, "Not to worry."

As we came in sight of the barge, Richard waved to us from his high perch and called out, "I was about to send scouts to round you up."

We hurried the remaining distance and on board. Sylvianne was waiting, rope in hand, ready to cast off. Linda called from the stern as we came aboard, "There's a long run ahead, Richard says."

The sun was warm and bright; it drew us all on deck after a few minutes of scattering to leave packages below and gather up materials for our separate occupations, knowing we would probably not employ any of them. We were scarcely reassembled when Bob the discoverer called out again. We had rounded a bend and were looking up at the château in the distance, a beautiful sight, but Sam had his own interpretation. On his feet immediately, in a Napoleonic or, more appropriately, lord-of-the-manor stance, he moved an arm slowly in a wide, expansive arc.

"Look at that, Mildred. We'll sit up there on the front porch—we'll call it the terrace, of course—and watch the barges go by loaded with our produce for the market."

"Sam," Mildred told him, "I think I'm a little nearsighted."

For the rest of the afternoon Sam was not with us except by physical proximity. There was little general conversation, but there was a sporadic communication of enjoyment of the sun and the passing scene: A very small boy with a very large dog driving a herd of cows along a narrow lane just beyond the towpath. A little farther on, along the same land, a farmer driving a two-wheeled cart and wearing the faded blue smock that is as essential in the French countryside as the fleck of red in a Corot landscape. A group of children waving and calling to us, each of them, boy or girl, wearing the black coverall as inseparable from a French child, except for Sunday best, as the blue smock from a French workman. These were some of the things we were pointing out to one another, not that the others were not seeing them too, but to imprint our shared enjoyment. Sam had no part in this; his eyes were on the horizon; his inner eye and heart had stayed behind at the château.

The shadows were long and the air was cold when we finally went below to change for dinner. When we came up again Sylvianne was on deck, the rope coiled over her arm. Richard had swung on the boom to the bank, and was driving in a stake for mooring. I asked her where we were. With a massive shrug for emphasis, she said she did not know, but she relayed the question to Richard. With another convulsive shrug, eyes and eyebrows raised to heaven, she relayed his answer: "We are near Biches." She

more boats over the winter for the coming year.

"She was absolutely charming," Bob contributed, "and furthermore would not take a penny for driving us." When I wondered aloud about the division of labor—did she do the locks and her husband all the boat-hiring business or did the husband alternate with her at the locks?—Charlton pursed her lips and shook her head reflectively.

"I don't think her husband."

I was indignant. "Do you mean she does all the work?"

"No," was Charlton's answer. "I just think he's not her husband. She kept referring to him as her partner."

"That's the French way," Sam informed us, and was bewildered by our spontaneous roar of laughter.

"It's not an exclusive, Sam," was Mildred's explanation.

Immediately after lunch we left the barge and took to the Volkswagen, driving Michel with us to do some marketing in Decize.

Decize, and I quote from the guidebook, is perched on an island of the Loire on a steep ridge—I am glad to have the guidebook verify it as a steep ridge—a little town made up of narrow winding streets, steep as the side of a mountain, rimmed by bridges across the Loire, and the canal.

We parked the car in a broad town square and scattered. Michel would have darted off like a dragonfly, but I caught the sleeve of his coat to ask where we would find him. He mumbled in an agony of embarrassment he would return to the car *de bonne heure* with his provisions. Remembering what had come out of the taxi on a previous marketing expedition, like the contents of the stateroom in the Marx Brothers film, Bob said firmly Michel must not try to bring back the provisions; instead he must speak, tell us where we should come for them and for him. After a great many protests that he did not wish to "derange" us, he conceded he would "return himself" to the car and then direct us to the place where he would have left his collected purchases.

Frances watched him move across the square, slim, graceful, with an unmistakable look of distinction.

"I still cannot picture," she said, "that young Byron married to our brawny tough Sylvianne, and"—turning to Sam—"don't tell me that's the French way."

Standing in the square, we could see on one side zigzag narrow streets going steeply up to a peak that from below looked as slender as the tip of a cone, and spreading over this like an eagle on its aerie, a church of such vast proportions we could not see its lateral extremities. With turrets and center spire increasing the height, the whole edifice seemed to threaten rather than bless the town. On the other side of the square we saw and moved toward—that is, some of us moved in that direction—a wide beautiful esplanade bordered on the river and the near side by a double row of plane trees, trimmed to a symmetrical umbrella shape. Along the *allée* they made, between the double rows of trees, groups of men were playing *boule* and further on little girls were squealing over a form of hide-and-seek.

At the far end of the *grande allée* between the rows of plane trees I saw a kind of enclosure and horses. Sophy was already at the enclosure with Bob.

"You were watching the men play *boule* when we passed you," the General told me, and Bob corroborated it.

"You had edged so close the players were stepping around you. We thought perhaps they had made you their mascot."

It is disconcerting, I find, to have my curiosity about people and activities observed by others.

We were looking over a fence that rimmed an expanse of well-kept grass. Tethered along the fence were magnificent horses, heavy Percherons, dray horses, farm horses, all of them so groomed their coats shone like rippling water in the sun, their heavy beautiful manes and tails combed as fine as the sheerest wool and plaited with colored ribbons.

Most of the horses were black, some gray; the halter of each one was white. A few feet away a small group of men lined the fence. I moved toward them to ask what was going on. It had been a horse show, they told me, a competition that had taken place throughout the morning. It had just ended; most of the horses had gone. I returned to the General and Bob with this information and then moved on across the *place* and up one of the narrow winding streets. High up one of these and quite out of breath, I came into a square like the one on the riverbank, although smaller. Standing there, heaving a bit, I could see for myself, and for the first

time, the actual formation of this island at what the guide-book called a crossroads of water channels—the Nivernais Canal, the Lateral Canal and the Loire River. The view was glorious and I was glad of a bench from which to enjoy it. Some time later, when I'd come upon other members of our band, I told the General I'd climbed all the way to the top to see the church.

"Whatever for?" was her comment and I could only echo it. The name of the church is l'Église St.-Aré, and the legend about the saint is more appealing than the place where he is buried. According to the legend, the saint, who in life was the bishop of Nevers, in death was placed by his own request on a barge, unmanned and set afloat in the River Loire; wherever it came to rest must be his burial spot. He was not buried, however, on the banks of the Loire but entombed in the church that carries his name. The guide-book points out that one of the few existing Merovingian crypts is to be found here, a statue of the Virgin dating from the sixteenth century, and also some bas-reliefs of the same date, together with, of course, the shrine of St.-Aré. These would be rewarding to scholars in that field and period, but other than its size, I found nothing to justify behaving at my age, as the General said, like a mountain goat.

"It is my considered opinion," Albert told us, panting a little, "that every citizen of Decize is a qualified marathon runner."

This pronounced judgment made more surprising the sight of shoes displayed in store windows. Charlton was the first to point these out as we straggled down single file, except for Albert, who held Frances's arm in a vise because her right ankle tends to fold over. As we reached in turn each window to which Charlton pointed, we passed back and forth gestures of surprise and emphatical lack of appreciation. I think I have never seen uglier models—thick-soled, stub-toed, with very high heels, in appalling combinations of leathers and colors. How women could walk in them, especially up and down these streets, was difficult to imagine; how they could choose them, impossible to believe, considering the French standard of chic. Clothes in the shopwindows we had noticed were smart and the women we had passed on the street well-dressed, smartly turned out. "However," Bob qualified, "I was not looking at their feet."

We relayed these travelers' impressions to Mildred and Sam, whom we found sitting on a bench in the esplanade. Halfway up one street, Mildred said, had been enough for both of them; they had returned to enjoy the view of the river and the activities in the *allées*.

Charlton drove us home to the barge with Bob on the seat beside her, holding a map because, they said, they wanted to make a few detours to show us the charming places they had discovered in the morning on the way from Mont-et-Marre. We gave full marks to their discoveries from the very first stop, actually a slow circuit of a little town called Cercy-la-Tour, pleased with its compactness of small houses, charming tidy gardens and relatively simple church. Bob did the navigating from his map, calling out the names of the villages we passed through.

When he said, "Here we are, Charlton," she slowed the car. We rounded a bend and faced an inn that could have been a mirage because of its incongruity in a setting of farmlands and the simple little villages we had passed. This was an inn, its modest hanging sign identifying it as such, to which the fashionable world would come for perhaps a weekend or a seasonal event. There were windowboxes all across the façade of the first and upper floors, each filled with fall blooms carefully tended. Behind the main building on one side there was a large garage, on the other an even larger stable, and we could see through an open door box stalls. The overall comment was of total disbelief in its existence there.

"Wait," Charlton said. "Bob and I think we found the reason for it. You'll see it in a minute." She drove on perhaps five minutes and stopped the car.

"Now look," she said, and we looked up one of the most magnificent *allées* we had ever seen in our lives, we agreed, with a double line of trees on the one side and a beautifully cropped grass footpath between, a single line on the other stretching seemingly interminably. That *allée* led to a château, whose details we could not see, only tantalizing glimpses as we drove beyond the *allée*. We rode farther on after a few moments of speechless wonder and delight, passing fields of cattle, and in the meadows beyond, beautiful creatures that were unmistakably race horses. As we sat watching these lovely animals, Bob expounded his and Charlton's theory.

"We think there's a racecourse somewhere on this estate, and probably, at certain times of the year, sales of maybe cattle or, well, colts. That's the reason for the inn—probably crowded enough at the time of the special event to make up for the rest of the year."

We acknowledged the logic of this and were loud in our praise of their discovery. Only Sam was silent, looking meditatively out the car window.

By what seemed to the rest of us a kind of sorcery, Charlton and Bob between them, with mutual certainty, agreed on a particular road, unmarked, nothing to distinguish it from any other country lane. We followed its winding course between beautiful fields of beautiful cattle in a wide smiling landscape. We were not talking, only breathing country smells and dreaming over the country itself. Suddenly Charlton called out, "There's our *péniche.*"

"My, my," Albert said. "Sure enough."

Seemingly in the midst of green fields we saw the roof of the *Palinurus.* Our home away from home was moving in its deliberate, quiet way along the canal toward our meeting at the lock.

We were vociferous in our loud cries of admiration. The driver and navigator, granting they had the help of a map, had chosen a road that brought us to the very nose, almost, of the *Palinurus.* Charlton stopped the car, we all got out, and by waving and shouting caught the attention of Richard and the others on board. Exchanging across the meadow congratulatory shouts of mutual discovery, we then drove on ahead to the lock, where we waited for the snail, the symbol of the *Palinurus,* to catch up with us.

While we waited we talked to the lockkeeper, as usual a woman, and it was an unrewarding and frustrating conversation. The great château, she told us—and without doubt she knew all about it, except that she could not at the moment tell the name of the owner, a very important man and with a title, *le comte de* . . . and she shook her head. *"Quelque chose."*

Sam spoke for the first time since we had looked up the *grande allée* to the great château.

"I don't believe it's a count anything," he said gloomily. "It's a Rothschild and he wouldn't be interested in my offer."

Chapter 11

At breakfast next morning each arrival was greeted with variations of "Do you realize we came on this barge a week ago today; does it seem possible?"

"In a way"—this was Bob's phrasing—"I think it was yesterday and in another way I can't think of a time when I wasn't on the *Palinurus,* just this endless tranquil slipping through the days, and I'd like it not to end."

For Sophy and Charlton that day was marked as unlike any other on the trip; at times it seemed endless, and unlike Bob, they longed for it to end. As they told it to us later I begged to have it written down; and this is Sophy's account:

"We left Isenay on the barge at quarter to nine; it was pouring rain. We reached Cercy-la-Tour for lunch (of course the day before by car it had been a matter of a few minutes). At three o'clock, although it was still raining, Charlton and I left the barge to look for a taxi in order to pick up the car at Isenay. Richard had suggested we go across the bridge, where we would find a café and surely a taxi. No sign of a café across the bridge, but a hundred yards or so up the road, finding one direction unrewarding and retracing our steps, we came to a café. I opened the door into a crowded smoky room, the tables filled with men and women; every table had four to eight or so people crowded around it and every one of them stared at us and not one of them spoke. Charlton muttered at me, 'Let's get out of here,' but I edged round the tables saying a placating *'Pardon, madame, pardon, monsieur,'* as I squeezed by. No one answered. When I reached the bar I asked the man behind it how we might find a taxi to take us to Isenay.

" *'Mais, madame, c'est pas facile; voyons, c'est dimanche.'*

"This was like setting a match to the fuse on a stick of dynamite. The room exploded into speech, offering advice, arguing with one another that the advice given was that of an imbecile, that the only practical way to obtain a taxi was —and this would provoke another argument. No overall agreement was reached, but the vote of the majority seemed to be that if we walked on down the street a few hundred yards we might possibly find a taxi, perhaps on the left, perhaps on the right. Charlton had not left the doorway and backed out thankfully when I rejoined her, shaking hands on the way with the nearest occupants of the tables I passed. We walked for I should say ten minutes along a deserted main street, but as we sloshed through puddles the rain stopped. Once or twice a small car whizzed by; no taxi; every house was closed and every shutter. As we were trudging past the closed gate of a house slightly larger than its neighbors, a thin, delicate-looking gentleman opened the gate and stepped into the road abreast of us, looking at us inquiringly.

" *'Monsieur,'* I said, *'pouvez-vous nous indiquer où on peut trouver un taxi?'*

"He sighed, *'Ah, madame,'* and his voice was thin and gentle, *'c'est pas facile aujourd'hui, comprenez? C'est dimanche et il y a très peu de taxis le dimanche.'*

"We realized this, I told him, but had he by chance any suggestion he might give us? For an appreciable time he stood looking vaguely past us, lost in thought. He sighed deeply before he spoke. Possibly the best thing would be to go to the station. My inquiry of the whereabouts of the station sent him into another pensive remoteness. Emerging from this, he told us with a sigh to continue straight along for five hundred yards, then turn to the right, and after two hundred yards we should without doubt come to the station.

"We thanked him, shook hands and started off again. Behind me I heard him sigh deeply, and I turned back thinking he had a message to add, but he had gone away into thought, standing in the road looking beyond us into the distance.

"When we turned right at the next crossing as we had been directed, we saw ahead of us a car parked, the first parked vehicle we had seen in the whole village.

" 'This might be a taxi,' Charlton suggested, and we walked a little faster though we were so tired by now, after the distance we had covered in wet shoes and clothes sticking to us, we only wished we had never left the barge.

"As we came abreast of the car a man came very suddenly from around the far side in front of it, standing without a word directly in our path. There was not another person in sight and we did not like the appearance of this one; his clothes were dirty, his complexion sallow and his eyes darting from one to the other of us seemed to me very shifty. He did not say *'Bon jour,'* let alone ask if we needed assistance; he said nothing. Rather than walk around him, I thought it better to explain ourselves, and I told him our problem. I think now that he was not sinister but soft in the head, because he continued looking from one to the other of us, still not saying a word. Charlton whispered perhaps he did not understand my French, but I told her that was impossible. This time it was a deus ex machina who rescued us. A little boy, bespectacled and about six years old, I should say, rode up on a bicycle, stopped and resting one foot on the ground, poked his face inquisitively between us and listened to my repeated inquiry about a taxi.

" '*Il y a quatre taxis à la gare,*' the young messenger said, and rode off.

" 'Four taxis at the station,' I repeated to Charlton. She had understood perfectly, she told me, what the little boy had said. What she did not understand was why we were standing there. 'Let's get away from this man.' He did not step aside, but he made no effort to stop us. 'Hurry,' Charlton said, and I did not look back.

"Drawn up along the station platform were four taxis; we counted them, agreeing they made the prettiest sight in the whole landscape we had trudged that day. We fairly pranced into the station and up to the ticket window and the man looking at us inquiringly from behind it. Where would we find the drivers of the taxis outside? I asked. We would like to engage one to take us to Isenay. The man at the window answered with a massive shrug.

" '*Ah, madame, aujourd'hui c'est pas facile, vous savez, c'est dimanche.*'

" 'If I have to be told again,' Charlton commented, 'that today is not easy, that it is Sunday, I just might have a kind of screaming attack.'

"The man at the window had more to offer. Perhaps if we would wait for a train that should come in at four o'clock, one of the taxi drivers might appear, in case a passenger required his services, but of course it was Sunday, we must understand.

"Thankfully we found and sat on a bench outside the station, regretting only that the train would arrive so soon, tired as we were. Individuals and small family groups came on the platform to wait for the train. I went to the other side of the station, asking each driver of a car bringing in travelers if this was a taxi and could I engage it. After the fourth indignant denial from a *père de famille* I retreated to the bench again, finding Charlton, in some agitation, on the verge of leaving it.

" 'That sinister man is here,' she told me. 'He must have followed us; he keeps darting up and staring at me.'

" 'I think he's just half-witted,' I told her. Her answer was she did not find this reassuring. I consented to leave the bench only in the hope a taxi might arrive with passengers or the drivers turn up to claim their cabs parked alongside the entrance. There was no sign of an owner of any of these, but a bus arrived, and when the driver opened the door to discharge passengers, I asked if on the return trip he would go anywhere near Isenay, and I explained our problem. After a moment's consideration he told us he could drop us three or four kilometers from the inn at Isenay and from there we might obtain a taxi.

" 'If we ever got there,' Charlton muttered, 'I'd spend the night.'

"The bus driver had another suggestion: we might go across the railroad tracks past a turnaround and down that road six hundred yards or so; that was where an ambulance found itself and there might be along with it a car with a man to drive us. We thanked him, and after we'd seen everybody off on the train and not one of them brought by a taxi, we trudged off once more, to look for an ambulance and a driver.

"At the end of our dismal plod across the railroad tracks, past the turnaround, down the road six hundred yards, we faced an empty yard and a closed garage. At that moment I felt this might be the end of the line for us. Instead of that luxurious inn we might just settle here and wait, for whatever time, until the garage was opened and perhaps the ambulance would return us to the barge.

"Charlton interrupted my speculation about the immediate future by telling me someone was looking at us from the window of a house across the road. I crossed the road, went up a path to the house and knocked on the door. It was opened by a young girl and behind her was a man as frail in appearance as the one at the very beginning of our trek, whom we had left standing on the road in dreamy abstraction. Once more I made my appeal, ending on a personal note that we had been told we might find an ambulance here. The young girl answered that certainly, indicating the gentleman behind her, this was the monsieur who runs the ambulance and certainly he would have been delighted to take you wherever you wish, but unhappily—with the familiar shrug—today was Sunday, we must understand. Then would by chance the monsieur, and by now I am convinced mine was as poignant an appeal as a door-to-door salesman ever made, would he have his own car, or did he know of a friend who had a car who for a price would take us to Isenay, because you see we had come on a barge and we had left our car at Isenay and now we had left the barge at Cercy-la-Tour and we had been looking for a taxi for one could not imagine how long a time. The frail gentleman answered my appeal. He assured me mournfully he himself had no car and he had no friend who owned a car but—and his voice brightened perhaps a half note—if we would go back into the main street and there turn right and go down about eight hundred yards we would find Madame Girard. Madame Girard had a taxi herself, *'bien commode.'*

"We took to the road again; the girl called after us on our way down the path and we waited for her message. While there was a sign, she told us, in Madame Girard's window that said on it TAXI, the sign was quite faint, therefore we must search carefully. We went back to the main street, turned right and proceeded slowly, looking carefully for a faint sign, eight hundred yards, nine hundred yards, a thousand yards. We had long since abandoned any efforts at conversation. A car came toward us, slowing down as it reached us, and the driver leaning out and leering at us was the sinister man with the shifty eyes. We went back over the thousand yards, looking, we thought, as carefully as bird watchers for a taxi sign, and the sinister man reappeared three times, always with the same performance. We had almost reached the bridge to the barge—Charlton was all for crossing it and handing over our torch for someone else to carry—when we saw coming toward us two very nicely dressed ladies who looked to be either taking a Sunday stroll or perhaps on their way to pay a call. One of them spoke, the first person who had volunteered a remark, and certainly it was the most soothing remark we had heard: 'Madame, could I by chance help you?'

"Charlton said afterward I looked as if I might burst into tears for an answer but I did say, 'Mesdames, we are looking for the sign of a taxi we have been told is somewhere on this street.'

" 'But certainly, madame,' was the answer. 'You have just passed it. You must retrace your steps some two hundred meters.' She took my arm, propelling me gently into the street and pointing. 'You see those turquoise shutters,' and I could see them in the distance. 'There you will find a sign, very, very faint. You must ring the bell and there you will find Madame Girard.' They had spoken alternately and sometimes together. I thanked them both with all my heart and we shook hands.

"Following their instructions, we retraced our steps and did make out, thanks to the turquoise shutters, a small piece of cardboard stuck on the wall of a very prosperous-looking house. The sign carried four beautiful letters so faint it was no wonder we had missed them. The letters spelled TAXI and if there was a bell at the gate it was as modest as the taxi sign. I could not find it, but the gate was unlatched. I pushed it open and walked somewhat timidly into a delightful courtyard, timidly because I am always fearful of a lurking watchdog. No dog, but a beautiful shiny new Simca car. There was no bell visible to me at the front door so I knocked. The door was opened almost immediately by a lady who was a well-tailored and efficient fifty, I should think. She said she was Madame Girard, had we come to engage her taxi? At my fervent endorsement of this, she suggested we get in the car while she procured her motoring coat; she would be with us in a moment.

"She returned, buttoned up in a smart driving coat, eased us out of the driveway and onto the road, pausing there to look in either direction. Satisfied, she set off at ninety kilometers an hour with the heat and the radio turned on full. She deposited us at our own Volkswagen, the charge was twenty francs and she was off again. We could hear the radio until she was out of sight. It had not taken her long to cover that distance. When we came on board the *Palinurus* Sam looked up from his book—you were all on the deck lazing in the sun.

" 'What took you so long?' he asked. 'Been doing the town?' "

Chapter 12

Albert and Sam developed a new activity on the barge, one that was confined and peculiar to themselves; no one else had the slightest wish to be drawn into it. They did their own laundry. Sam was the instigator, not surprisingly since he has been a producer and promoter for the greater part of his life. That his creative imagination and energy should be turned to washing out his underwear was a surprise, particularly to Mildred, since, she pointed out, during the whole of their married life she had never seen her husband dip so much as the toe of one sock into a washbasin. Now he would come hurrying up the stairs, holding in front of him a wrung-out something, not so wrung that it did not shed a trickle of water to mark his path. Albert was usually close behind him, Sam calling back exhortations to step it up, they must get their wash out to dry in case of rain. It did rain almost invariably and almost within a few minutes of the spreading out of the wash. Pointing out to them this phenomenon of nature, we urged they abandon this fever-

ish course, because when they were not involved in it, the sun shone, but let them display their accomplishments, the clouds gathered and broke. Acknowledging this but refusing to be dampened by it, each wore his hat and overcoat for the hanging out; Sam was the more active of the two laundrymen, going frequently to inspect it, bringing it in if the sky looked ominous, replacing it when he felt he had been overcautious, only to repeat the cycle. When we left the barge for excursions, the laundry was consigned to Linda to hang in the stern. "And," Sam always added, "keep watching it." The result was that from the bow we might present quite a stylish appearance, but from the stern the look of a tenement in a particularly depressed area; then the appearances would be reversed.

Mildred found all this disturbing, she said, making her feel off balance. "First I see women operate the locks, then I see two men with real talent in their own fields running back and forth with their coats on, carrying their wash."

Hearing this, Bob looked up from the book he was reading. "They're playing *Tobacco Road*," he told her.

Charlton reported to us Linda's comment: "The men really need not have this compulsion about laundry; it would all be taken care of."

"As a diversion," Charlton added, "she intimated there were things she could enjoy more than Mr. Hackett's and Mr. Jaffe's wash flopping about her." Sam waved away this reflection on his activity and skill.

"Linda is a dear sweet young girl and a pleasure to look at, but I don't feel she puts her heart into laundry."

Linda *was* a dear sweet girl, not shy like Sylvianne and Fabienne, but self-effacing, with charming manners, conveying a feeling of wanting to be helpful but never intrusive. I could see she got on well with the two French girls. Once, coming back to retrieve something from the barge before setting out on an expedition, I had come upon her setting Sylvianne's hair, with Fabienne looking on and the three of them laughing together. Linda, however, was not from their background, that was obvious, but what hers was I could not guess, and I was curious about it.

The day after Sophy's and Charlton's pursuit of a taxi, I woke with a cold, just the beginnings, I reported to the others. If I stayed at home and for the greater part of the day in bed, I was sure I could stop its going any further.

"It's not that I'm not sorry," was the General's comment, "but I do think it's odd that Charlton and I tramp about for hours in the rain and you come down with a cold."

At about half-past nine (I was not near enough to hear the General call out the exact time), they left in the Volkswagen to visit Sancerre. When they had gone, Linda came down to fetch my breakfast tray and asked if she could do anything for me. On the instant I knew what she could do and this day was heaven-sent for satisfying my curiosity.

"Yes," I told her, "there is something I would like very much for you to do if you are willing. Not laundry," I interjected quickly at her look of surprise. "Fabienne does ours beautifully. I want you to tell me about yourself, the things you've done and the things you want to do." She said if it would not bore me she would be delighted. We agreed when she had finished her jobs I would be dressed, and we would meet upstairs and talk. I was not disappointed; this is the story she told me.

Linda's father and Captain Richard's mother were brother and sister. Linda was born in East Anglia just outside the little town of Havershill. She had passed her twenty-sixth birthday on this trip; she had no brothers but one sister who was thirty. Her father was an engineer and inventor; one of these inventions, a special grinder for lawnmowers, he and his brother manufactured. As she talked affectionately of her sister and her parents I sensed a very close and understanding family relationship that included great fondness for Richard's mother. She had seen much of her aunt and of Richard, particularly when they were little children. After the usual preparatory school —she did not specify which one or what sort—Linda had gone to a college of home economics, with two possibilities in mind, she said: either to be good housekeeper as a wife, or to make home economics a career. Graduating from college, she had done cooking for a year in an institution, "but I did not feel this was creative, stirring mammoth pots and decorating the icing on little tarts." She left that job and went to Switzerland. "I wanted to learn German, so I went to the German part. I worked in a hotel; it was a very small hotel high up in the mountains and very beautiful; I loved it." When I asked her if she had cooked there, she laughed.

"I did everything—cooking, cleaning, a little gardening, chambermaid work. I did enjoy myself and it was very good training and very helpful for learning German."

She did not tell me why she had left the little hotel; she only said next she had gone to Basel, working for a family with five children. Again, she said, "I did everything," enjoyed it all and found it very helpful to her German. "Except that the children spoke what they called Schweizer-Deutsche, which was a kind of patois as far as I could understand. When the children spoke this, their parents corrected them and that was a little confusing. I was never sure which one I was using."

"To this day," she said, and laughed, "when I am speaking German I can see by the expression on the other person's face I have been using Schweizer-Deutsche." She laughed, "They look so surprised."

"What about friends? In between cooking and scrubbing and taking care of five children, did you meet any of your own age and sort?"

"One or two," she admitted, "not many, but I had a

126

hobby. Bells. You hear them and see them all the time in Switzerland, every size, shape and period, so I started making a collection. One of the nicest things to happen to me was because of my bells." She was glowing at the recollection. "There was a very old man"—I wondered what her definition of very old was—"who had an antique shop. I was poking around in it one day and I saw a very old bell; it was beautiful, the shape and the tone of it. I began talking to him and we became real friends. I used to go to see him whenever I had time off and we would talk and talk; he was very interesting and I always looked at and held the bell.

"One day he told me if I would take it away and polish it—it would be a very hard job and take a long time but it would show that I really loved it—then he would consider selling it to me. How I worked over that polishing, and every time I went to see him he would ask how I was coming with it. Finally one day I brought it to him. I was leaving Basel and going back to England to be with my family for a while. He looked it all over and said I really did love it because I had done a good job of polishing it and so he was going to sell it to me. My heart was really pounding because I had not been paid very high wages and it was going to take almost all I had made to get back to England. I was going to be embarrassed to have to tell him, even if it was for him a low price, I could not buy it. And do you know what he said?

"He said the price would be one Swiss franc. He knew I could not have accepted it as a gift, but all he said was, 'I told you I would sell it to you and I am selling it to you.' Wasn't it a lovely thing for him to let me have the bell in that way? It is one of my very special treasures."

She had gone back to England and after a little time with her family had taken a job with a friend to work for a woman who had "a very big house on a very big estate." The two girls had done all the cooking, "every day and large parties"; their employer was charming and went out of her way to make things pleasant for the girls.

"What brought that to an end? You obviously are not still there."

"I needed more education. I'd specialized in home economics, and talking to our employer, the lady of the big house, I realized more and more how little I knew of anything else, so I went back to college."

"In England?"

"Yes, at Bury St. Edmunds. An aunt of mine lives there and I stayed with her."

"What courses did you take?"

"English literature, some biology and quite a lot of history. I love history."

"Did you have any life outside the college?"

"Oh yes, my aunt has many friends and wide interests. One of the nicest things we did was madrigal singing; my aunt is a very good musician and she drew around her a group that loved to sing madrigals. There were quite a few dons at Cambridge who used to come over for a weekly session; it was the greatest fun." Her face saddened. "There was another activity I got very involved in, but it was not fun. Not very far from Bury St. Edmunds there was a camp for displaced Indians from Uganda; they had been evicted after Idi Amin, the dictator, had taken over."

"Was it a large camp?"

"There were over two thousand and so little provision for them it was shocking. We were so few volunteers we didn't seem to make any dent at all, and yet we worked frightfully hard and they were so grateful it was heartbreaking."

"Was it too much for you? Did you have to get away from it?"

Linda was shocked. "Never; I would never have left them, but the camp was disbanded. The situation is very much better; the commission in charge found friends, relatives that would take them, so now they're scattered throughout England and they're among their own kind."

Linda looked directly at me, quizzically but a little shamefaced.

"Back to home economics after all that extra history and things, but a friend had bought a restaurant and wanted me to go into it with her. That was really hard work; we did everything including Sunday teas, so there wasn't even a half day off. I really had to give that up."

"After how long?"

"A little over fourteen months."

"And then?"

"Let me see, I think that was when I took a secretarial course, that is, typing and shorthand, and it's been very valuable in a way. For a time I worked in a bookshop; I think between the typing course and my job with an American firm. It was in the personnel department and everyone was terribly nice but six months of it and I was completely fed up with indoor office work."

"Did you head for the woods?"

"I rented a house, a little house, in Bury St. Edmunds and I really had a wonderful job there. I drove a delivery van and I adored it. You see, I made my own hours. It was a firm that delivered fresh linen and collected the supply that had been used; it was a hire plan and they supplied everything for hairdressers, shops, and offices. Every Friday night I would be given my route for the week and I could map it out in whatever way I wished. I covered almost all of East Anglia."

"But you left?"

She nodded a little ruefully, I thought.

"Well, yes, I did, only this last July."

"Surely you weren't tired?"

Her large eyes widened even more with astonishment.

"Oh, dear, no; that never happens to me. Actually it was just that I felt stagnant. You see, it wasn't like being abroad. I had friends there, not just in Bury St. Edmunds but all over that part of the country. I used to see them quite a lot because, you see, in this job I had more time off than I'd ever had in any other. Almost all the friends were married and had children by now, and being with them gave me a very odd mixed feeling. In a way I felt they had great fulfillment; there wasn't a single couple that wasn't making a go of it and a good one, but I was aware at the same time of how confined they were. Here I had gone to a college of home economics with two ideas, as I told you before, one to make myself a good wife and housekeeper and the other to make a career of it. Well, suddenly I realized that being a good wife was exactly what I did not want to be. I didn't want, at least not now, to be a wife at all."

"You haven't said anything about how your family felt when you took these kinds of jobs."

"They've been simply wonderful; I can't tell you how sympathetic they are, no matter what I've been doing. Of course, I would never do anything to hurt them."

"Did you get in touch with them when you decided you wanted to see more of the world?"

"Oh, Miss Kimbrough, I've never been out of touch with my family. You do understand, don't you—we're very close."

Understanding was the quality I certainly would have applied to her parents, I thought, but I did not say so.

"My family thought it was a splendid idea to see more of the world, and they suggested I try to get in touch with Richard. That did seem a good idea, so I went off with a knapsack and an address book to catch up with Richard somewhere. The London office wasn't much help. I got in touch with it; the people there said they really could not tell exactly where he might be." Remembering my own com-

munications from that office, I was not surprised. "So I hitchhiked my way along the canals, the rivers, having a frightfully good time exploring the country, and sometimes I'd ask if anyone had seen the *Palinurus.*"

"He must have been thunderstruck when you finally did reach him."

"Not really. As a matter of fact, I hadn't been asking recently, so I came upon it near Dijon quite by accident, tied up along the bank. Just as I saw it really was the jolly old *Palinurus,* Richard came on deck, so of course I hailed him from the bank."

"Did he fall overboard?"

"Why, no; why ever would he do that? He simply asked if I was planning to join him. I said, yes, I was, and he said, well, then come aboard."

"How long do you think you'll stay?"

Linda frowned. I'd never before seen her face tighten sternly.

"Actually there's a difficulty I never thought of, nor did Richard. I've talked about it with him; it's the Algerians. They annoy any girl who is alone. I want so much to see all of France. I was going to have a traveling companion, a girl from home who isn't married either and was longing to travel, but now, if you can believe such a thing, she's got herself engaged."

"So what will you do now?"

"I shall go on, of course; there's so much I want to see."

She was like a child at the moment, putting her hands to either side of her head to make a balloon shape. "I only wish the top of my head would open up and get bigger so that I could absorb even more, but"—with a shrug and a return to a mature steadfastness—"I have to walk with my eyes straight ahead, never looking to the left or the right. Sometimes I feel like a horse wearing blinders, but"—and she was very serious—"although I'm physically very strong I wouldn't dare try so much as to brush off an impertinent hand. A friend of mine who was hitchhiking in France like me did just that, no more, only brushed a hand away. The next minute she was upturned and on her back, with a hand around her ankle, all in one quick turn. Fortunately she was able to scream and was not assaulted."

There were other things I wanted to ask her, more personal than factual—her human relationships, had she had an affair—but I sensed in her a dignity of reticence that would have considered my intrusion into her privacy as unwelcome as the touch of an Algerian hand. We talked a little longer in a desultory way; she had very much enjoyed the variety of people that made up passengers on the *Palinurus* cruises of the season.

"It was interesting too to see how quickly they made friends among themselves, and even as small as our passenger list is, how soon they made up smaller groups of some special mutual congeniality. Some were cardplayers, some were tremendous walkers, others were on bicycles the greater part of the day, some were tremendous sightseers wanting to go to anything, any place within reach that the guidebook recommended. Richard would provide a car for them. Others just wanted to poke about at whatever place we were moored, and of course there were always some ladies who asked first off about the shops. But I do think it's interesting that we've never had a passenger who got bored and wanted to leave before the end of the cruise. I must say usually the cruise is one week."

For the last half hour or so as we'd been talking I had been aware of Fabienne at the head of the stairs down to the kitchen peeking round at us, but I had not wanted to be interrupted. Linda, however, intercepted a look between us when I shook my head, and jumped to her feet.

"Oh, I've kept you so long talking about my family"—which was not exactly the way it had been. "I do apologize. I know Fabienne wants to bring your lunch." When Fabienne had gone to report this, I held Linda a moment longer to ask how she got on with the staff.

"Oh, we've become great pals. We have lots of things to talk about and Michel isn't nearly so shy when he's off duty. Do you know he and Sylvianne have a little boy two years old. They do love him so, they have pictures and pictures of him, and he is adorable, but he has to stay with Sylvianne's mother while she and Michel are working; she simply longs to get back to him and so does Michel. They're a very close family."

"Where will they go when the season is over?"

"Straight back to Sylvianne's mother and the baby, and then next winter they hope to have a job in a restaurant and have Sylvianne's mother and the baby with them; that would be wonderful."

"They won't go away on a trip?"

"No." Linda shook her head rather sadly. "I'm coming to think this is a French characteristic. French people don't seem to want to travel, they don't really care about places outside of France; they even think travel pictures on 'les flicks' are boring. I can't understand it."

"Just one more minute, Linda. What about Richard's girl?"

Linda, on her way to the kitchen, turned back and came toward me, shaking her head.

"I don't really know. She seems even more shy than Michel and yet she's very sweet. She's always willing to help, in fact she asks to, but there isn't anything really for her to do. Richard has made their quarters very attractive and she stays up there the greater part of the time. Now I must really go and not hold you up any longer."

"You're a very polite girl, Linda," I said, but she did not hear me.

Thinking later about our conversation, I knew there had been nothing about it to let me say, "Now, you see, that's your English girl today." In the first place, I do not know English girls so I have no standard of comparison; in the second place, I cannot fit Linda's pattern to any environment of country or class. Here obviously was a conservative middle-class family producing in Linda a sport and not disconcerted by it. I had reached that point of speculation when I remembered Richard, the first cousin with the same background. I had had a similar conversation with him on our earlier trip on the *Palinurus*—my " 'satiable curiosity." He had been sent by his family to the Sorbonne to learn

French as one of the preliminaries to becoming a journalist, but he had preferred boats and canals. By means of a legacy from a relative, not his parents, he had bought and remade the *Palinurus,* and now in addition had two other boats, I think. How long he would continue the barge life no one could foretell, least of all Richard, but he would never go back to journalism. I had heard him say that was one thing he was "dead certain" about. Through all his vagaries his family had been steadfast and sympathetic, he had assured me of that, surprised that I'd even asked, and I remember his having told me that early on, when he had not been able to afford staff, his brother and his brother's wife had helped for a while, even though the brother, a substantial business-man, had thought the whole project lunacy.

So—I was talking to myself—what price this British stiff-backed insistence on, almost religion of, conformity? Richard's family and Linda's had been able to give each of them a good education, they must be at least comfortably off, yet they had sent her with address book and knapsack to go hitchhiking. My inability to learn anything about her love life piqued and confused me as much as the paradox of her family conservatism and tolerance. In our conversa-tion, coming as near as I dared to probing, I had asked her if she'd ever been in love. Those expressive and honest eyes had widened again.

"Oh, no," she said. "Never. I'm not sure that I shall ever marry," which was not exactly what I had had in mind. Later, relaying her story to Mildred, who is satisfactorily as curious about people as I am, I said, "I'd be willing to wager Linda has never had an affair, and I'm equally sure she likes men very much. I've seen the way she is with Richard, who of course is old hat to her, but also with men we've seen along the way, walkers and bicyclists on the towpath, stopping to talk. Far from being shy with them, she enjoys them. When I asked her about Richard's girl she

135

took that situation completely in her stride; she wasn't in the least censorious about it, felt no necessity to make excuses or apology, but, I repeated, "I'll bet she's never had an affair of her own."

Late in the afternoon the travelers returned. I had gone to my cabin after my late lunch, had a nap, and feeling my cold had retreated to distant thunder on the far horizon, was on deck looking for them.

The day had been an unqualified success.

"No," Sam said ruminatively, "qualified. We went to Sancerre for wine-tasting and it tasted awful."

"Unqualified for me," Mildred answered, and her voice was lilting. "We didn't see a château."

During the drinks before dinner, from every member I had the full story of the expedition. Their first destination had been Sancerre. We all knew and very much liked Sancerre wine; now they would not only visit its source, but taste it.

"What about the wine-tasting?" I prompted.

"Just a moment," the General requested. Evidently she had taken over the chairmanship of the testimonial meeting. "We haven't got to that yet. Bob, you tell her about the place you directed us to."

Bob obliged. "I knew there was a little place called La Charité, before getting to Sancerre, I wanted them to see. I'd been there once a long time ago and I wanted to visit it again myself. I don't think anyone was disappointed?"

Frances nodded emphatically. "One of the most beautiful, in a way, places I've ever seen, and it was certainly the most unusual. Tell about it."

Bob resumed. "Along the river side there's a street, more a road actually. Crossing that, you come to a square, little houses around it, and directly ahead of you is the church. Actually it's the Basilique Notre Dame, a magnificent ruin of Burgundian Romanesque architecture. It had been at one time a Benedictine abbey, an offshoot of Cluny. It was called one of the daughters of Cluny, and the place has had quite a history. The name itself, I remember reading the first time I was there, dates from about the eleventh century. When travelers, pilgrims and the poor came to the abbey for help or lodging, the hospitality and the generosity of the friars became so widely known the word was passed about, '*Allez à la charité,*' and since the phrase referred to that particular abbey it became the name of the town, La Charité."

Frances, with an apology, interrupted. "But tell why it's so extraordinary now."

Bob obliged again. "You walk up the nave of the church and you realize first that it has no roof and then when you look on either side, instead of seeing separate chapels you are looking at separate dwellings. When people first began to take up residence there I have no idea. How it's come to be allowed I couldn't tell you; I only know that in that church today there are many dwellings, with people living in them, and that's La Charité today, consecrated in the twelfth century."

There was a great deal more I wanted to ask, but obviously the other testifiers were impatiently waiting their turn. Later in the guidebook I read considerably more about La Charité, and it was rewarding. The place was scarcely a Johnny-come-lately. At the beginning of the eighth century it knew an era of great prosperity until an invasion by the Arabs. Later, because of its situation on the Loire, it was the scene of a struggle between the Armagnacs and the Burgundians during the Hundred Years' War. Joan of Arc laid siege to La Charité.

Frances had said what an extraordinary place La Charité was. I found it equally extraordinary that in all the description in the guidebook there is not a mention of the tenement life existing today within the walls of Basilique Notre

Dame. It might have been worth noting that La Charité had come full circle and was providing hospitality and a haven again.

Sam was impatient. "Tell about the wine-tasting," he urged, and without waiting for any urging continued the recital himself.

"We were driving along flat country, fields, pastures on both sides, and then we see ahead of us hills, and as we get closer we see they're solid with vines. So now we're coming to the vineyards, and I'm beginning to think about the wine we're going to taste. Mildred reminds me it's like the country around the hill towns we've seen in Italy, but my mind is on the tasting. We come into the town itself and it's all narrow winding streets up and down hill with little stone houses that are right on the street, and on nearly every one of them there is a sign. I could read the signs, of course, but you'd better tell, Bob, what they said."

"Vins à déguster," the General prompted.

"That's what I would have said." Sam commended Sophy's contribution. "You know the way we usually scatter,

but for some reason this time we were all together. I knocked on a door and a nice-looking woman opened it, seemed about fifty maybe, and a younger woman behind her, her daughter, they looked so much alike. I didn't feel like talking French at the moment, so I turned around for Bob and that's where I saw we were all of us bunched there. I think it was Sophy though, not Bob, who asked if we might come in and taste the wine. They told us to come right in; they were very hospitable. We walked straight from the front door into the kitchen; it was fairly large but we crowded it. There was a big pot of soup on the stove."

"I never smelled anything so delicious." This from Charlton.

"And the room was lovely and warm too. It was pretty brisk outside and we'd all got sort of chilled on the drive, but my mind was on the wine. The mother led us out a door on the far side of the kitchen; we had to go single file; we looked like a snake line on the football field after a game. The lady took us down a few steps and there we were in a cellar, only it was separate from the house."

"A *cave*," Bob amplified, "*cave*, a wine cellar."

"That's right," Sam agreed. "Well, she took some glasses from a shelf, nice generous-size wineglasses. She wiped out every one of them as she handed it to us and then she filled each one of them from a barrel. I waited until every glass was filled and that was real sacrifice; my tongue was tingling by that time. I lifted the glass to the mother and her daughter and my companions and at last I drank, and never in my life have I tasted anything as close to raw vinegar."

Bob interrupted with a convulsive bray of laughter and apologized. "I'm sorry, Sam, but as long as I live I'll never forget the expression on your face. Expression? Expressions! I never saw so many so fast—astonishment, dismay, your lips puckered up, your eyes starting out of your head, the big swallow, your effort to be polite, the sickest smile I ever saw on anybody and the look you gave to the remainder of that glass of wine. I know you were struggling to say something polite but what you said was 'Jesus!' "

Sophy broke in. "And the woman said, '*Merci mille fois, monsieur,*' and dropped a kind of curtsy; she was terribly pleased."

"Well, I was terribly pleased"—Sam was unmistakably smug—"the way I bowed her ahead of me, got you all into snake line again, and poured out the rest of my glass." He smiled through the barrage of indignation this admission provoked; obviously the others had suffered a full tasting.

"As a matter of fact," Sophy commented when the babel had subsided to low muttering, "I don't understand why that wine was so bad; either the year was a poor one or it hadn't been aged sufficiently." She turned to me. "The place was more than a little touristy, all those signs inviting wine-tasting and the number of inns in a town of that size, every one of them with a sign about the wines they served, so the town must bring a lot of tourists in the summer, but the tourists here are people who like wine and know about Sancerre. I'm sure we just struck a bad year or a bad *cave.*"

"Do you want me to go on with the story?" Sam asked, and continued immediately. "When we got out of the house—and I think perhaps I did give her an impression we would be back to buy a little of her wine—"

"By your gestures," Charlton interpolated, "she must have guessed at least a dozen cases."

Sam ignored the interruption. "Then we walked around for a little while and we were hungry. I kept remembering that pot of soup and I wanted to get the taste of that wine replaced, but we couldn't decide which one of the inns to try. Frances decided for us because she saw in front of one of them a delivery van that had such a charming sign, she said the inn it belonged to must be good."

"I copied the sign for you." Frances hunted in her bag.

No wonder they had followed her plea for the Auberge Mellot. The inscription she had copied from the delivery van of the inn read, translated: "Alphonse Mellot, Wine-growers and Distributors from Father to Son since 1513." Evidently some members of that long line had enlarged the winegrowing industry to owning an inn.

Sam endorsed the decision. "I knew it was going to be good the minute we walked in. Most of the tables were occupied and all the people at them were French; wher-ever the French are you know the food is going to be good."

"Why didn't you get into conversation with them?" Charlton asked with wicked innocence. "They seemed ter-ribly interested in all of us."

Sam reproached her. "I don't butt into other people's conversation." He allowed no time for an answer to this. "I was right and Frances was right; the food was fine. They gave us a table in the center of the room and showed us a hatrack at the far end, where we hung up our coats. The food was not great but close to it. As for the wine, beautiful. Took away the taste of that awful vinegar at the house and did a lot more. We tried both the red and the white. We brought back the case Richard asked for and a surprise, two separate bottles for you."

"It *was* to have been a surprise, Sam," Mildred reminded him.

Sam was discomfited but only for a short minute. He rallied. "Well, Emily, register surprise."

Registering and expressing surprise, pleasure, gratitude, and to sidetrack further recriminations, I urged someone to tell me the rest of the day. Albert obligingly and hastily filled in.

"We left Sancerre right after lunch and we got to Nevers.

We scattered there as usual; Frances and I had some things we wanted to look for."

"Nice postcards?" I asked.

"Lovely," was Frances's answer.

"What about the cathedral," I prompted, "and the old gate and the ducal palace? I did my homework in the guidebook."

There was an embarrassed silence.

"Well," the General said after an appreciable pause, "to tell you the truth I didn't feel like sightseeing." There was an audible sigh of relief. "I just wandered and poked about. I met up with Charlton part of the time; she was doing the same thing." The silence that followed this was an eloquent admission that they had all done the same thing. Bob broke the silence.

"Well, I did hunt up some things," he apologized.

"Thank goodness," was my response to this. "Somebody elevated or at least kept up the 'ton' of the group."

"That's just what we said to Bob," Mildred admitted shamelessly. "He wanted us to go with him to the cathedral and to another fascinating church he knew about. Sam and I encouraged him to do it for us. You're an obliging fellow, Bob, dear."

"Well, the cathedral was very interesting," he said, directing his report to me. "The others don't deserve to hear about it, the slackers. It includes two separate and distinct styles and periods at either end; I've never seen anything quite like it. One is Western Roman and the other is Eastern Gothic, and the dates jump from the tenth to the sixteenth century. It's not all that beautiful, I have to admit, but it's fascinating."

"Go on, Boy Scout," Charlton suggested, "tell her more of your good deeds while we slackers were just rambling."

Bob, pausing to make a face at her, which she returned, continued. "The Church St. Étienne is a gem. It's all of a piece, pure English Roman, eleventh century. It's austere and beautiful."

"The guidebook calls the façade sober." I apologized for interrupting. "It was an unusual word to use and to come upon in the middle of French and spelled in the English way too."

"Absolutely *le mot juste,*" Bob approved, "and the interior is sober too, not all cluttered up with statues, but the stone itself is a soft beige, almost gold, really beautiful. I tried my best to get the others to see it, and they were willing because they were in the car by that time and I promised them they wouldn't have to get out, only look at that 'sober' façade."

"You mean they balked even then?" adding I was shocked at their backsliding.

Bob averted a thundercloud of protest.

"I couldn't find it," he said. "Damn it, with all those one-way narrow little streets I couldn't get back to it. In the end I had to give up and we drove home."

"So disappointed," Charlton told him sweetly, "we could have cried, we had been so looking forward to it. I think it was generous of us to forgive you so quickly when you admitted you couldn't find it."

Bob turned to me.

"You never heard anything quicker, like a trained chorus. Not one voice off key asking me to keep on trying, full chorus as one voice: 'Let's go home.'"

As I was getting ready for bed that night there was a knock on my door, so faint had I not been hanging things up on the other side of it I would never have heard the sound. I opened the door to Frances.

She held out a bulging paper bag.

"I didn't want to disturb you, but would you like to see our postcards?"

Chapter 13

To be aware on a barge of a sudden increase of speed from three to perhaps six kilometers an hour within a very short time is irrationally alarming. On the morning after the excursion to Sancerre and Nevers we were still dawdling over breakfast and conversation at nine o'clock. Mildred and Frances were having both in their cabins; we could hear them talking back and forth. We had not breakfasted so late on any other morning, each one coming up to the lounge apologizing, with the explanation he had been so exhausted from the day before he had overslept.

"All that sightseeing to churches and cathedrals," Bob said with a straight face, "did us in."

Sophy and I at the same instant realized the increase in speed, looked up startled, catching each other's eye and remembering simultaneously another time.

"In the car in England?" she suggested, and I nodded. That had been years before along the Thames and British canals on our first barge trip. That time we had not slept aboard, but each night had been met by a car and driven to the local inn, where we had reservations. At the end of the first day, when the car had picked us up—we were five on that cruise, and had driven only a minute or two—all five of us had called out in shrill agitation, "Slow down—are you a racing driver?" The look of stupefaction on the chauffeur's face as he turned his head toward us I shall never forget.

"I'm just at twenty," he had said. Difficult to explain to him how it felt after a long day of doing three.

The others were less than a minute behind the General and me. Each one of them looked up and at one another, startled and alarmed.

"What the hell's going on?" was the way Albert phrased it.

Mildred called from the foot of the stairs: "Sam, go see if Richard's fainted; he's lost control."

Richard, strolling into the lounge, overheard this and stopped over the stairwell.

"Quite all right, Mrs. Jaffe. Everything's under control. We've got such an easy straightaway, Sylvianne's doing the navigating."

"I'll tell Frances," was Mildred's rejoinder. "She's getting dressed fast for whatever the emergency is. I don't think she's planning to jump or swing off on the boom, but she's prepared."

At our invitation Richard joined us for coffee and told us more about our run and speed.

"The run is long today, something near forty kilometers, but there are very few locks and it's quite straight."

"Seems to me," was Sam's objection, "we've been on a straight before, but we didn't change pace."

Richard agreed. "The difference is between the other canals and this one. You notice we're out of the Loire and into the Loire Canal. This canal services a lot of industrial plants; when you go out you'll notice other barges all along. They're loading and unloading gravel and other freight, so because it's business these canals are kept in very good condition and the locks are operated efficiently. You'll notice I'll be charged and given a receipt for every one we go through. The other canals, almost all of them, are entirely for pleasure craft—and that means very little traffic, so you get indifferent lockkeepers who don't bother to maintain a water level or keep the lock machinery in good order. There ought to be a constant communication among them so that the water level, starting, you might say, at the top, would be maintained all the way. Instead of that, as you've seen, we've had to stop each time for the water level to be reached for our need. That makes the going slow." He laughed with quite a French shrug. "And sometimes we get mired. We've been lucky so far, only one little spot of poling." He should not have said that.

Looking out the windows for the first time—when croissants, jam, marmalade and two large china pitchers, one of coffee, the other of hot milk, were in the immediate foreground there was never any interest in a more distant view —we realized we were in unfamiliar surroundings. What had been gentle countryside, except on the day of dark forests and tunnels, was giving place to signs of industry and commerce. We went on deck for a wider view and thought very little of it. We looked with disfavor, and said so, at the barges loading and unloading, factories, people and, worst of all, noise. For more than a week the only sounds we had heard from the barge were the chatter of reeds along the bank when our gentle wake stirred them, a far-off crow of a rooster, the bark of a dog, the bray of a donkey. This sudden cacophony was as great a shock as our sudden acceleration of speed had been.

"Get us out of this," we urged Richard. "Take us back to those winding, inefficiently run canals."

Richard was soothing, promising we would be back to our quiet ways very soon. We were approaching a lock as he was pacifying us and we crashed into the side of it, interrupting his sentence. As we clutched one another for support, trying at the same time to avoid two deck chairs that had overturned at the impact and were sliding about wildly, Richard continued talking, with a slight change of subject.

"That will be Guy," was his explanation. "He came on board last night, going to run with us for a couple of days. He's taking a hand at navigation, alternating with Sylvianne. Obviously he's at the wheel now. She wouldn't have done that. He's a newspaper fellow."

Richard moved away toward the stern, not hurrying, and calling back over his shoulder, "I want you to meet him."

Sam called after him, "Aren't you going to see what the damage is?" and Albert, simultaneously, "I'd better get Frances. We might be stove or is it staven in?" And Sam again, "You'd better look to your prow, man."

Richard paused, turned around, nothing in his face to show either appreciation or dismay over these nautical terms. "Just a little paint scraped"—he was still reassuring —"at that angle. I'll just take over now."

Had I been asked to testify to it, I would have sworn we had all gone on deck, but returning to the lounge I saw Charlton and Bob placidly reading. Sam went immediately toward the kitchen. His laundry was at the moment in the stern, he explained; he wanted to make sure the bump had not shifted it. Albert went to the head of the stairs to reassure Frances, who was calling up to know if we were aground. Sophy asked Bob and Charlton if they knew we had a stowaway on board.

"A *what?*" Charlton evidently did not know.

Bob nodded. "I met him last night. He came aboard after you had all gone to bed; Richard introduced him. He's a very pleasant fellow, on holiday from his newspaper. He's French but he speaks perfect English. He's a great pal of Richard's. Richard wants to persuade him to go into partnership so they can alternate running the boat."

The General voiced the opinion of all of us: "If his steering doesn't improve, I don't want to be on his alternate run."

Mildred came up the stairs carrying a book and her needlework bag. Since Sam had not resumed bicycling, her paraphernalia had decreased. She signaled me to join her in a far corner, and when we were together asked where Sam was.

"In the back," I told her, "talking to the girls and seeing to his laundry."

"That will keep him for a while. I want to talk to you about Sam and this idea of going to live in Paris for six months. I know he told you about it; he admitted that to me. Has he said anything more?"

"Once in a while," I told her, "he's mentioned it, but not recently."

"That's a good sign. Maybe he's tapering off. But I want to tell you, Emily, this is the first time I've taken one of his ideas seriously, and I can tell you I'm worried."

When I told her she hadn't looked it, she nodded.

"If I opposed it by so much as a look out of my eye, that would be all that was needed to push it through. I know my Sam, and I don't need to tell you I adore him. I went to Africa with him when he was making *Born Free*. It wasn't the easiest trip I've ever made but it was interesting. I moved to London because that's where he wanted to be, and I have to admit I love it. But what in God's name would I do in Paris? I don't speak the language, I don't even understand it very well, so the theatre would be practically out for me, sitting there like a dummy. Of course I love pictures and museums, but not day in and day out. And shopping?

Dressmakers? They're torture to me; I'd rather be strung up by my thumbs than stand for fittings. So I'm telling you now and I told Sam, but I don't think he believes it for a minute, for the first time since I married him, and that's a long time, I'm not going to leave him but he's going to leave me behind in London. I'll do without the pleasure of hearing him surprise the natives with his crash-course French."

Sam came up the stairs from the kitchen, carrying a bundle that was not compact; odd socks and a shirttail trailed from its parts.

"I'm going to shift these to the front," he explained. "I think it's more to windward." Mildred, hearing him on the stairs, still talking had moved from our corner. I think she did not want him to suspect she had been confiding an anxiety.

"I bought a London *Times* yesterday in Nevers, and I left it here, I think. Has anybody seen it?"

"Mildred," Sam told her, "do you know we've got a new passenger aboard? The girls have just been telling me about him. He's a friend of Richard's—are you listening?"

"Certainly I am."

"Well, that's not satisfactory. You're walking and I don't want running shots; I want stills."

"You tend to your laundry," she advised him. "I'll hear about the man later."

"Yours to command, Queen," and he went on deck with his bundle of wash.

The surprises of the day had not ended. While we were having an apéritif before lunch, Richard brought his friend into the lounge and introduced him.

"This is my friend Guy Bardet." He seemed a charming young man about Richard's age, with pleasant manners. He shook hands, repeating each name, as Richard went with him through the group. He spoke beautiful English with only a faint accent and was at ease while we talked for a few minutes, though neither he nor Richard would join us in an apéritif.

When they had left we discussed for some minutes the possibility of a partner, agreeing that he seemed an admirable choice.

"Just needs a little more practice at the wheel," was Sam's modification. The *Palinurus,* we agreed, was too heavy a responsibility for Richard to carry alone, even with the splendid brawn of Sylvianne beside him.

"You know," Frances told us, "Richard has had a very bad cold the last few days. I've been urging him to drink a lot of brandy. Suppose he got really sick." She shook her head in anxiety. "I don't like to think of Albert taking his place at the wheel."

"With the amount of brandy you're suggesting," the General observed, "I doubt there would be much difference."

The day did not lend itself to excursions in the Volkswagen. Richard, answering a halloo and inquiry from Sam calling up to him from the deck, had said there was nothing particularly rewarding in the vicinity and furthermore it was raining. Sam, reporting this, added he hadn't needed Richard to tell him it was raining.

The day was fulfilling the all too frequent weather forecast in the London *Times,* one that I have always considered the most wistfully optimistic prognosis I have ever seen given. "Bright intervals anticipated," those reiterated forecasts read.

We were having bright intervals just long enough for us to settle on the deck, only to be driven in again. By the middle of the afternoon we abandoned the effort as not worth the trouble and were all settled in the lounge, some reading, the Hacketts and I playing Scrabble and Sophy wrestling with our accounts.

On every trip Sophy has been the treasurer, sommelier and general tour director, meticulous in each of these roles, though we have urged her not to be so fussy about the accounts. This was not because at any time any of us was indifferent to the expenditure of money, but because of the system we had agreed upon on the very first trip and subscribed to on each succeeding trip and group. We did not go through the finagling tedium of itemized accounting, involving such exasperations as "You took coffee but you

did not have orange juice; there are three desserts on the bill, who did not have any?"

Such pettiness, we felt, could give rise to lifelong enmities. Therefore, our system was for the General to take charge of an overall pot, each of us contributing to it a stipulated amount, she to pay from it all common expenses, telling us when the pot needed replenishing. Nevertheless, and in spite of our protests, she insisted on keeping strict account of all money disbursed and showing this to us. That afternoon in the rain belt she was sweating in a corner to the accompaniment of muttered swearing, with enough words audible to show it was swearing and not in a happy mood. Bob had the temerity to ask if he could help her; this was the first trip he had ever taken with her, and that was probably why she answered him politely and with restraint.

It's those two bottles of wine bought for Emily, . . . she told him. "The case of wine was ordered at Richard's commission and paid for, but I can't put the cost of the two bottles into the pot since Emily is a contributor to the pot and this was a present to her."

Overhearing this, I urged her to forget about the present and put me in the pot.

"It was a lovely idea," I assured those listening, "but I don't suppose you thought I was going to drink up two bottles of wine alone in my cabin, so for heaven's sake just make the idea a present and let it go at that."

Sophy asked everyone to listen and repeated this.

Only Frances demurred. "It's such an ungracious way of making a present."

"Frances," the General said earnestly, "the opposite is going to be a very ungracious way of sending me right round the bend."

Frances hastily withdrew her objection.

Late in the afternoon we not only slowed down our hurtling pace of six kilometers an hour; we stopped. We assumed we were coming into a lock, but Sam opened the doorway to the deck, explaining he liked to keep a close watch on the operation of the boat and be available if needed for consultation.

He reported, "We're not at a lock; we don't seem to be anywhere in particular; I'll have to investigate." He gathered up from the lounge and put on overcoat and hat—his laundry outfit—and went outside.

Mildred was on her feet at the instant of Sam's announcement, running the length of the lounge and snatching up a coat she had dropped on the bench inside the door at our last retreat from a rain flurry.

"I don't trust him," she called back as she bolted through the door. The Hacketts and I had left the Scrabble board, and almost simultaneously the others were moving toward coats and the deck. To our delight we were in time to see Mildred clutch with both hands and in a most undignified manner the rear of her husband at the moment he was extending himself across the deck rail, obviously in order to grasp the boom, that had been released, push off from the rail and swing to shore.

"Are you crazy?" Mildred was demanding rhetorically, and Sam was struggling for liberation. We happy spectators were shamed by Frances. With a Valkyrie's cry she elbowed us from her path to Mildred and implanted a grip just above hers. This turned the tide of battle, Sam capitulated and Frances was herself again.

"Oh, Sam, dear, please forgive me. I thought Albert might try it again."

Sam, able to stand upright once more when the two women had released their tentacles, resumed command. "Get me ashore. Where's Richard? Bring the gangplank."

Linda's soft voice came from the stern. "Righto, Mr. Jaffe. We're just putting it down."

Our attention had been so spellbound by Sam and his attendants we had not been aware of other activity. Now we saw Sylvianne and Guy on the shore. Obviously they had used the boom, and with the heavy rope and Sylvianne's strength now pulled us close enough to the bank for the gangplank to be put down. I do not know who had carried the spike and the great mallet, but Guy had got the spike a little way below the surface and was endeavoring to drive it in. I daresay few things in his life up to then had made him more unhappy than the sight of us trooping down the gangplank and surrounding him, to watch the mallet after mighty heaves from the shoulder pound the earth on one side or the other of the spike. Now we were all asking the whereabouts of Richard and no one could tell us.

"He went off on the *Mobilette*," Linda vouchsafed, "at a lock about two hours ago. He had some business to take care of, he said, and I heard him tell Sylvianne and Guy to tie up around five o'clock wherever we were and he would find us."

Sylvianne called out, "Monsieur Quelconque"—she never learned our individual names. Bob, Sam and Albert started toward her, but Sam turned back.

"I'd better help with the pile-driving," he explained. "Her French is a little unfamiliar to me." Sophy and I followed the two men.

If someone would take over the rope, Sylvianne requested—she had got the barge so well into the bank it was only a question now of holding—she would drive the stake. Bob and Albert took over the rope she relinquished and Sylvianne relieved Guy, obviously to his great relief. Sylvianne suggested Guy lash a little more tightly the rope at the stern she had secured round a distant tree trunk. There was not a tree easily available to the bow rope; this was an absence we had not been aware of, nor had Guy.

"I didn't realize trees were a part of navigating," he admitted with a grin and charming candor.

At times since we had watched her initial effort Sylvianne must have been practicing, because she swung around and over her shoulder the iron mallet and brought it down unerringly on the head of the spike, unerringly except for a few hair-raising interruptions, when Sam, supervising, leaned down to see how far in the spike had gone and Sylvianne by swinging her whole body around avoided his skull.

Once we were firmly attached fore and aft and Sam had pronounced everything shipshape, we went back not to the lounge but to the deck. The sky had cleared, the wind had dropped, the air was warm and there was a beautiful sunset.

"Out of the rain belt," Albert said, and reluctantly, as the glow in the sky faded, we went to our cabins to change for dinner.

Chapter 14

"I don't know when I have left a place
[Digoin] with so much joy."
DOUGLAS GOLDRING, *The Loire*

The morning after our ensemble mooring, Guy left us. We
were having breakfast when he came into the lounge with
Richard to say good-bye. At our expressions of regret and
hopes we had not driven him off by a certain levity of the
day before, he assured us his departure had nothing whatever to do with the few lapses from his otherwise perfect
navigating, but because his holiday was ended and he must
get back to his paper. Bob asked politely if he might hope
Guy and Richard had made an arrangement for the future
and Guy's answer was that it was very probable, but now he
had a suggestion. Richard was taking him on the *Mobilette*
to his, Guy's, car. Surely we would like to pick up our own.
He would come back here and chauffeur to our own car
whoever wanted to pick it up.

By the time he returned Mildred was dressed, in the
lounge and eager to go with Charlton, she said, to pick up
the Volkswagen. "Gives us a chance to talk about all of you

and maybe do a little shopping."

They met us at Dion, where Richard had told them we would tie up for lunch. They had had a full and satisfying morning, they reported, "just poking around," doing a little shopping and then driving about the countryside in a roundabout way to Dion. They intended to count this their excursion of the day. Now they would settle in for the afternoon with their needlepoint and talk.

Immediately after lunch the rest of us took to the road by way of the Volkswagen, the General at the wheel. The morning travelers had told us they had passed a fascinating group of buildings and around them an extensive walled area of farming land. They had not stopped because they were afraid they would be late for lunch, but Charlton, who is her mother's own daughter, told us precisely how to find it and her mother found it precisely. What we all found out very precisely was that this large estate was the Abbaye de Sette-Fons and that women were not allowed to set foot within its outer gates. Frustrated though not chastened by our rebuff, we retreated, muttering to one another our disapproval of such isolation, an isolation that excluded us. We did not know the origin of its name and I have not yet discovered its meaning. We circled the very considerable acreage, all of it enclosed within stone walls. Across the fields we could see members of the order working.

Digoin was our objective and specifically its château described in the guidebook as a beautiful residence of the eighteenth century with two façades of quite different architecture, the principal one fronted by a large courtyard that in turn was entered by a magnificent wrought-iron gate. This courtyard was flanked on either side by two projecting pavilions. The façade looking out on the park (it was built in the early part of the eighteenth century) "is centered by a portico two stories high and at either end a cylindrical tower topped by a cupola." This was a mouth-watering plum to reach for, and we reached it, thanks to the General, unerringly. A modest sign beside the outer closed gate read NOT OPEN TO VISITORS.

We were not only frustrated by this rebuff, we were a bit chastened.

"Aren't we welcome anywhere?" Bob asked himself aloud.

"Shops," the General answered him gloomily, "but who wants to shop?"

Frances and Albert spoke simultaneously and in bright voices: "Postcards?"

No one responded to that proposal.

The Hacketts left the car at the corner of an obviously shopping street. We would retrieve them at that same corner in half an hour. Half an hour later we were still trying to find that corner. Every street was narrow, winding and one-way, and every street corner looked precisely like the one selected for our tryst. Sophy repeated until it became a refrain, "It isn't possible, this is ridiculous."

The chorus from Bob, Sam and me ran: "Try this street, I'm sure that's the corner, no, I think we just passed it. You can't back, of course, we'll have to go round the block."

It started to rain. Actually it did not start, it came on full and suddenly.

Bob said, "I looked at the sky a minute or two ago and it was bright blue."

We found the corner and the postcard collectors just under half an hour *beyond* the time appointed for the rendezvous. They had of course reached it at the moment appointed and they were drenched but happy, each carrying a bulging paper bag. Frances apologized to Sophy for selecting a corner so difficult to identify. Albert assured her the wait had not seemed long at all, it was so interesting. Part of it they'd spent sheltered in a doorway watching people go into a movie across the way that was showing—

they had had a little difficulty translating the title, but were pleased when it turned out to be a picture they themselves had written years before.

Then we lost the lock. We asked separately, except Sophy, at least six people where we would find the lock at Digoin. Each of four people approached gave directions totally unlike the others'; two or perhaps three people with a heavy shrug said they had no idea. By this time we were outside the town, traveling muddy lanes just as narrow and winding as the streets had been, the rain as heavy as when it had started. We were climbing one of the steepest of these thoroughfares when Frances called out sharply, "I see the canal. Over there, on the left. We've just passed it." At this moment we were passing a farmyard. Sophy promptly turned into it, to the noisy dismay of a considerable flock of ducks and chickens, backed into the roadway and slid down to the foot of it. Frances was right. We had not recognized our familiar waterway because here it was a water bridge, passing over and high above a tumbling river beneath. The river ran swiftly under some seven or eight stone arches that formed the support of the canal bridge. Sophy parked the car at the side of the road and we went out into the rain because, as Sam said, "I never saw such a sight as this and I want to see it."

On either side of the canal, instead of a towpath we saw a broad sidewalk such as one would find on a city street, except that these sidewalks were bordered by wrought-iron fences.

"Probably the local citizenry promenades here of a Sunday afternoon," was Bob's speculation, but Albert saw and pointed out excitedly what was at the far end, a lock, and once he had pointed it out, we recognized the small building alongside as a lockkeeper's cottage.

Albert immediately announced his intention of taking his own promenade, but on the run the length of the sidewalk,

and getting from the lockkeeper directions for reaching him by car. He was dissuaded from this, almost forcibly by Frances, persuasively by Sam, Sophy and me, who pointed out between the end of the sidewalk and the lockkeeper's cottage a considerable gap of water without even the provision of a boom. Our final argument, to which he yielded, was that in this drenching rain it was unlikely the lockkeeper, snug in his cottage until the arrival of a barge, would hear even the loudest halloos if Albert tried to project his voice across the gap.

We went back to the car and sat in it soaking and shivering until the General announced redundantly we didn't seem to be getting anywhere. She followed this observation with the suggestion that we try without guidance to find our way to the lock. Almost anything, we agreed, was better than what we were doing, and we moved onto the road and up the hill again. Twenty minutes later we were back in the same spot. Almost immediately we had lost sight of the canal and, very shortly after, all sense of direction on the winding roads. We took no pleasure in our recognition of the spot we had so recently quitted, but we felt no incentive to try again. We were so wet and so cold we were sunk into a despondent apathy. Once Frances suggested to Albert they look over their postcards.

"Later," was Albert's answer. "I don't want to take my hands out of my coat pockets."

Once the General said, "We can't stay here all night." No one answered that.

A woman came from behind a building a few yards beyond our parking spot. At some time during our vigil Bob and Sophy had looked for assistance there. The embodiment to us of Florence Nightingale, Joan of Arc and all the saints came directly toward the car. She was wearing a raincoat and hood. Sophy rolled down her window as we all leaned toward her like a field of wheat in a wind.

She told us she had been watching us from the window of her little house directly behind the machine shop she indicated—this was not the time to query the General and Bob about the reason they had not gone round the building at the time of their visit to it. We had been in this spot so long she had begun to wonder if our car had broken down and if we needed help about repairs. Her husband owned the machine shop and was at home in their little cottage. Sophy and Bob, I saw, did exchange a quick look but there was no comment. Sophy explained about the barge, our need to find it, and Bob supplemented with a report of our unsuccessful search for a road that would take us to the lock.

It was difficult to find, she assured us, but if we attended carefully and followed the directions exactly, we would have no further trouble.

Obviously the barge was not at that lock, we pointed out to her, or we would have seen it. She agreed; then undoubtedly it would be at the lock preceding the one within sight, but when we reached the nearer one we would find a road alongside the canal and following that would certainly come upon the barge.

To say we thanked her would be a Popocatepetl of understatement; we flooded her with gratitude; we begged her to accept some form of remuneration. She accepted only the former, urging us to be on our way and mind her directions. By following them, and we said them aloud along the way like children reciting a lesson, we turned off at a place we realized we had passed times almost beyond counting. The reason we had passed it was that it gave no appearance of being more than a scarcely discernible track across a meadow.

"I would have thought we were trespassing across somebody's farm," was the General's description. But it led us to the canal, a road alongside it and in the not far distance at long last a view of our Promised Land. We saw the *Palinurus* snugly tied up for the night at the lock beyond but at no great distance, not more than a mile from the one that had for so long been within our view.

As we drew alongside it and Sophy turned off the engine and we wondered aloud if even then we could reach the haven, cold, wet and stiff as we were, a lockkeeper came out from his cottage on the opposite side. We could not stay there, he shouted, waving his arms; this was a road and we were blocking it.

"I'm either going to kill him or burst into tears," the General said. "It's a tossup." She compromised by shouting back at him, joined by Bob, what did he wish us to do?

"If he tells us to go on or go back," Bob supplemented, "I *will* kill him."

"I'll be there with you," was Sam's grim rejoinder.

In the tumult Frances made herself heard, urging compassionate understanding because the man seemed so upset about something. By outshouting on our part, persuasion, and the rebellion of his own vocal cords, he was reduced to coherent demand that we come to his side of the canal by way of the bridge between, a sharply humpbacked structure so narrow Bob said afterward he would never have set the wheels of the Volkswagen on it. Skill, and I am sure despair at the alternative prospect, gave the General steadiness and courage. She took us over the hump and to safety and a haven on the other side.

The uproar had brought Charlton and Mildred to the doorway of the lounge. They welcomed us with indignant complaints. They had been very worried; why had we taken so long to reach the barge? Where had we been?

Each of us I think counted ten before answering and then Sam's response was brief.

"Mildred," he said, "for the present just say hello."

Sophy, after perhaps another count of ten, was a little

more loquacious: "For the last eternity or so we have been looking for you or sitting frozen and soaked in an ice-cold car."

"Why didn't you turn on the heat?" was Charlton's rejoinder.

"The what?"

"The heat, Mother. You get it by pushing down that little button on the dashboard that says 'Heat.'"

Chapter 15

Paray-le-Monial, according to the guidebook, is second only to Lourdes as a center of religious pilgrimages. The core of these pilgrimages is the order of the Adoration of the Sacred Heart and its inspiration is Ste. Marguerite-Marie, who as Mother Marguerite-Marie Alacoque founded the Adoration of the Sacred Heart; she died in 1690, was canonized in 1920. The basilica that was eventually consecrated to her was begun in the twelfth century.

On the afternoon following disaster day at Digoin we visited the Basilica de Sacre-Coeur and other places in the town of Paray-le-Monial. We had come that morning from Digoin by barge and reached Paray-le-Monial at lunchtime. The air, thumbing its nose at yesterday, was soft and warm, and Michel, sensitive to our moods, gave us a cold lunch to remember. It included a ring of tuna-fish salad, a dish of what I thought were sardines but was told were tiny mackerel, a tomato salad with a wonderful herb sauce, and a tray of cheeses, among them for the first time on the cruise the one I love best of all, Le Petit Suisse, which I can rarely find at home, and all of this so attractively presented Sophy took a picture of it.

We had reached a stratum of civilization that provided a telephone; by means of it a taxi was summoned. Charlton and Bob went in it to retrieve our Volkswagen, reporting on their return they had been sent on their way by the lockkeeper with unspeakable imprecations and waving arms.

On this excursion no one stayed behind, and we were still a solid body at the basilica we found well worth our pilgrimage. The distinguishing features of its exterior are the simplicity of its façade and at the same time the dramatic effect of its towers, punctuated along their height by beautiful arched windows. There is an immediate sense of the dramatic, too, in its interior because of a height that is truly awesome. Perhaps to emphasize the dignified austerity of the architecture, it allows no distraction by color or ornate design.

Once out of the basilica we separated as usual, going our ways on foot. The ways were steep, winding and narrow. At the head of one of these I found myself facing a façade of such contrast to the exterior of the basilica it seemed to me at that instant a kind of flamboyant immodesty, and I relished it. I was looking at the Hôtel de Ville, which one guidebook identifies as an historic monument of the sixteenth century. According to another guidebook it was not built as a monument; it was a town house built in the early sixteenth century by a prosperous citizen who was a Protestant. His brother, a devout Catholic, was so outraged by this shameless display of wealth he built a church directly opposite in order to hide the view of such vulgarity. Both brothers were ruined financially by their efforts. It is interesting, though not significant, that the church was destroyed during the Revolution, the town house survived.

The whole town was a delight—charming little houses, a swatch of garden through an iron gate set in a wall, sometimes from the head of a street a view of the canal below

and always from every level a sight of the towers of the basilica. For most of the time I walked alone; occasionally I passed other members of our band and our common salute was "Isn't it lovely?" I saw and admired the St. Nicholas tower of the sixteenth century, rampant with turrets and gables. I went into and almost immediately came out of the museum, partly because I saw nothing at first view to tempt me further, mostly because my legs were tired. Evidently the same affliction had occurred to the other members at about the same time, because we returned to the car by ones and twos but almost simultaneously. We came home to roost with no difficulty, either of finding our roost or of parking the Volkswagen. We were on our way below to change for dinner when Bob called to us from the deck.

"Look," was the only thing he said when we joined him, and there was nothing more to say. Against one of the most beautiful sunsets I have ever seen rose the great towers of the Basilica de Sacre-Coeur.

There was a saying in other times that *partout où le vent vente, l'Abbaye de Cluny a rente,* that is, wherever the wind blows, the Abbey of Cluny is collecting income. I think nothing could have given me a more stabbing realization of the rise and fall of the mighty than to come upon that saying after we had been to Cluny.

Before our excursion there on the day after our expedition to Paray-le-Monial, I had read the abbey had been founded in 910 by the Duke of Aquitaine, that by the end of the twelfth century the Clunisian order had included some twelve hundred monasteries scattered "from Poland to Portugal" and so many thousands of habitant monks no accurate poll was ever taken. Physically, in its architecture and interior treasures, it epitomized the best in taste as well as magnificence, though even then there was harsh criticism leveled at its luxury. Spiritually it represented equally the best of man's character—protection of the weak, hospitality and charity toward the poor and the promotion of peace among nations. The decay began in its spiritual world by an overbalance of trappings and luxury. One writer said, ". . . a bishop could not go even the distance of four leagues without the accompaniment of a suite of sixty or more horses." Another bitter critic said, "At Cluny a candle will not shine unless it is in a candelabra of gold or silver."

The physical aspect was the result of an actual demolition during the Revolution. What we wandered among were souvenirs of magnificence. We walked the length of the Grenier as it is today, only one-third its original size but with the great arched, ribbed ceiling intact. The storage house for grain now holds only random shafts of Corinthian pillars salvaged from another part of the abbey, long since gone. For all its fragmentary detail, the overall size of Cluny remains overwhelming. Passing one of our group on individual explorations, I would ask or be asked, "Have you seen the cloisters?" "Have you gone up the glorious outside stairs?" "Did you see the great staircase from the cloisters?" "Did you go to the lower room in the flour tower? A magnificent ceiling but there are only bases of pillars or statues around the floor." When we reassembled at the car everyone was declaring vocally his exhaustion. When questions were repeated there of "Did you see . . . ?" and the answer was negative, it was given with a snarl and the assertion that nothing on earth would induce a return to it, no matter how magnificent the sight.

The sight of food was the only thing that could draw us and we clamored for it. Bob with beautiful forethought had asked in the entry office (where Frances and Albert were buying postcards) for the recommendation of a good restaurant. His beautiful forethought, however, had not extended to making a reservation. I have never experienced such a scathing, lofty, contemptuous rejection as that given by the proprietor to our little band of waifs.

The following hour—it seemed longer—was one of misery and roaming. The General was at the wheel. Goaded by exhortations from behind her of variations on "Food, James, and don't spare the horses," she bumped us up one cobblestone street and down the next, but nowhere was there sign of a restaurant.

God bless the Hôtel de l'Abbaye and doubly bless its proprietor, Monsieur G. Beauford, who not only admitted but welcomed us. Even the other guests nodded and smiled as M. Beauford led us among them to two tables hastily put together and cheerfully reset. The food was excellent, and that did not surprise us. As Bob said, "What else could one expect? After all, we are in France."

The wine we drank, at the General's suggestion, was local. We had deferred to her because she is in charge of that department. She had told us dubiously, perhaps we ought to try the Mâcon, the white Burgundy of the region, though, she added, she had drunk it at home and had not found it worth recommending. Bob urged that we give it a try; he thought he remembered having drunk it and liked it. Prompted by this endorsement and out of gratitude to the proprietor, we ordered Mâcon. For all its earthly home in the vineyards of Mâcon, to us it came from the table of the gods on Mount Olympus. We smelled, we sipped, we sighed.

"And yet," the General admitted after a moment or two of inarticulate murmuring bliss from each of us, "I still wouldn't recommend it at home. Evidently this is one of those wines that don't travel well."

"Then," Sam offered decisively, "we'll just have to come back to it."

We went to Mâcon immediately after lunch. It had been on our itinerary from the start of this day's excursion, because Richard had told us Mâcon was a place large enough for cashing our traveler's checks and changing our money, since our cruise was coming to an end. On the way Frances explained her deep satisfaction at our destination.

"I think it's lovely and so appropriate that after enjoying their wine so much we should exchange our money at their banks."

The way to Mâcon from Cluny was, we agreed, the most

beautiful overland trip we had made. There are hills between, and every curve on the winding road brought a new and more expanding view. Because Cluny had been the cultural objective of the day, Mâcon the practical, not one of us, we admitted, had looked in the guidebook for what, other than banks, Mâcon could offer. Rounding the last bend with shamefaced surprise, we looked down on houses with round-tiled roofs and an overall vista of a charming town nestled along the bank of the River Saône. The General protested somewhat truculently that certainly she knew it was on the river and what river, but had to admit she had no deeper information than Mâcon's geographic location.

When we had extracted money from the Mâcon bank, and after a hasty perusal there of our guidebooks, we separated to explore. I looked for and found the museum, because, I read, the building was the one-time Ursuline convent of the seventeenth century. I was rewarded by the façade, but I did not go inside. Some of the others later reported visiting the ancient Cathedral of St. Vincent. They knew very little of it remained but Bob wanted to see its octagonal towers. Everywhere were reminders of Lamartine because Mâcon was his birthplace. I saw and read a plaque marking the house where he was born and felt on the instant a little as if I had been with Alice and the Red Queen, because eleven days before I had seen the château at Monceau where Lamartine had been and paid little attention to the notation in the guidebook that his birthplace had been Mâcon, a few miles distant from there. I had been traveling eleven days to catch up with our starting point.

With unerring precision the General, Bob beside her, navigated us, as designated by Richard before our departure in the morning, to the place of rendezvous with the barge. The drive there was almost as beautiful as the route from Cluny to Mâcon. To our regret and chagrin we had had to cut short the stay at Mâcon because of the time. The late-afternoon sun was warm, the air was clear, the country-side lovely in the soft light, but we dared not loiter.

"Here's the Ciry-le-Noble lock," Bob announced, looking up from his map and pointing, "but," he added, "where's the barge?"

Sam pierced the silence that followed.

"Well," he said in a small voice, "it's not raining and we know now how to turn on the heat."

We left the car to stand at the lock, making desultory suggestions of what to do, each of them trailing off.

"What is that?" Frances demanded, pointing up the canal.

"Well," was Albert's answer, "if it's not the Loch Ness monster, it's the *Palinurus.*"

It was not the Loch Ness monster. In less than an hour the *Palinurus* had reached us and we were aboard, with only a few wistful regrets that we had hurried. After cocktails, dressed in our best, we swept in, that is, across the lounge, to the captain's dinner, with Richard presiding, Sylvianne and Fabienne serving and Michel peeking at us from the top steps to the kitchen, dodging back out of sight at each compliment we tossed to him.

He had sent us first cold fresh salmon so attractively presented we pelted him with praise. Our response to the tenderloin of beef, browned minuscule potatoes and string beans caused him almost to fall backward down the stairs in his eagerness to get out of hearing. In deference to our insistence on no sweets for dessert he had provided a bowl of juicy pears, and apples and a tray of cheeses. When we started for bed, incredulous to find it was after twelve, Bob put his seal of approval on the day.

"This has been as close to perfection as mortal could hope for, building up to a climax, you might say, from Cluny to cheese. Now we'll just taper off, and a good thing too."

174

Chapter 16

We did not exactly taper off, we went aground. At Montceaux-les-Mines. We had arrived there shortly after lunch
and, told by Richard we would stop for about two hours,
had gone ashore. We had not found the town rewarding,
dismayed rather to find ourselves being jostled and shoved
by crowds of shoppers on a Saturday afternoon in a busy
mining town offering second-rate merchandise garishly
displayed.

Sophy, when in my ramblings I discovered her, was ex-
amining a rack of workmen's overblouses. "Comfortable in
the garden or on the beach over a bathing suit," she explained. Bob was with her. The others, she said, when she
had seen them were on their way back to the boat. That was
my objective too, and I left. By this time it was late afternoon, the sky was overcast and the air was chilly. I went
below, got a coat and came up on deck to see Sophy about
to come aboard, carrying a package she waved at sight of
me.

"Got the workman's blouse," she said, adding, "Has Bob come aboard?"

"Not to my knowledge," I told her. "Surely I'd have seen him. I thought he was with you."

"We separated. He wanted to get some perfume for presents to take home."

As we talked we realized simultaneously our engine was running and we were moving. Sophy tossed me her package. "I'll have to find Bob."

We had docked alongside a pier so there had not been the warning sound of our little gangplank being pulled up. I wanted to halloo to Richard to stop but Sophy flouted that.

"We'll walk to the lock, it's no distance, I can see it, but if Bob comes back to the car parked up there in town he'll wait there for the rest of us." She was shouting the last words because we were moving midstream and it was a sizable stream, not the narrow canals of other days. There on that day, Saturday the fifth of October, in midstream we stuck. We backed, we churned the water, but we did not move. This time we were too far from shore to be dislodged by a pole.

The General, Bob and the lockkeeper at Blanzy rescued us. They were not exactly the United States Cavalry but to us they represented just that. Sophy and Bob had not gone by car, horse or bicycle; they had walked, half run, to the Blanzy lock, a distance they admitted later was considerably greater than it had looked to the eye from the dock at Montceaux-les-Mines. Arriving there, they had called the lockkeeper's attention to the dilemma of the *Palinurus* in midstream. The lockkeeper's response had been that he was well aware of it, and it was a very stupid place to be. Bob's testimony afterward was that by ingenuity, persuasion and insistence the General, like God in *Green Pastures,* "passed a miracle." She suggested, she persuaded and finally ordered the lockkeeper to open the gate, pointing out that because obviously a boat had just gone through, his lock was full. If he would open his gates, releasing that spate of water, the *Palinurus* would be released.

"And that," I will tell my grandchildren, "is how we floated into Blanzy, though our captain was sore abashed."

The day had still more tapering in its program before we could say, "Now the day is over," though certainly "night was drawing nigh," and colder and darker. The General, admitting to being mortal, wanted nothing so much, she told us later, as warmth, rest and a drink, but Richard urged her to walk with him back to Montceaux-les-Mines, where he could telephone arrangements for the car to take the Hacketts and Bob next morning to Paris, then he and Sophy would bring the Volkswagen to Blanzy to be on hand for our own departure.

So the General had trudged back on foot with Richard to Montceaux-les-Mines, waited while he telephoned and driven back with him to Blanzy. Then she had her drink. The day had finally tapered to a close.

Chapter 17

Like the first cruise on the *Palinurus,* this one had begun with lunch at Fontainebleau, and this one ended where we had lunched on the first cruise, at Auxerre. Leaving Blanzy, we were not what my father used to call the full strength of the company. We were reduced, by the departure of the Hacketts and Bob, to Mildred, Sam, the General, Charlton and me. The Hacketts went direct to Paris in the car that had brought the Jaffes and Bob to the *Palinurus.* We were in the Minibus on our way to Orly.

Only the General and I had been to Auxerre; therefore on our approach to the city neither of us could count on support in the somewhat acrimonious clash of opinion between us.

Sophy was all for driving along the near side of the river as we approached it, and I would not hear of it.

"Keep going," I said, and when she demurred, I insisted, "Nonsense, just trust me for once."

Her protests were voluble, emphasized by reminders of

my inadequacy at maps and directions.

Acknowledging this, I offered my own reminders. "You know how it's been before. Granted I'm hopeless about reading maps, you have to admit once I'm in a city, I have a bird-dog sense or something that takes me to the hotel or whatever we want; in a strange city you unerringly arrive at the slums. Now turn right."

As we drove along the road on the far side of the riverbank I pointed out another bridge. "That's the one where we moored and the swallows flying around and under it turned copper in the sunset. Keep going. There it is."

"By God," the General said, "you're right. Who would have believed it?"

We parked the car, crossed the road, I modestly and unconvincingly disclaiming any credit for leading the way.

The restaurant was run by a woman; I had remembered that, but she had not remembered us.

"You have no reservation? Well, then, madame, certainly there is not a possibility."

In my individual pattern I have discovered there is no tapering. A moment of triumph is invariably followed by a stubbed toe. Nevertheless, I rallied from this ignominy and flung myself upon her sympathies. I told her we had been there six years ago, and hurried past her obvious indifference to this. I said we had always remembered it, that this was the end of another trip, it was unthinkable we should be turned away from this culmination after waiting six years. However, we would be happy to wait longer if at the end of it we might have a table. She melted; she had not the heart, she said, to turn us away under the circumstances. If we would go next door to the hotel and have our apéritifs there she would telephone us when a table was available, although, she warned, it would be at least an hour to wait. The others I somehow felt were not so jubilant as I at this concession, but reminding one another they did not know any other restaurant in the town and even more importantly it was Sunday, they subsided.

We were welcomed next door by the owner of the hotel, a Madame Quelconque—I have forgotten her name, but we learned she was the sister of the proprietress of the restaurant. She was charming, hospitable, her sister had already telephoned we were coming, she would take our order for apéritifs.

Though I have forgotten her name, my memory of her appearance is vivid, because when she had left the room we talked about the elusive quality of chic that is inherent in the Frenchwoman. She was wearing a gray skirt, a gray pullover sweater, a gaily colored scarf tied with a flourish and adroitness difficult to imitate. That was her costume and we said was it the cut, was it the scarf that gave such simplicity that indefinable chic? Sam said he thought we looked very chic, and we thanked him for his gallantry.

After our apéritifs, leaving word we would be back in time to receive our telephone call, we explored the city, scattering as usual. We had gone out all in one mood; we came together again as differently affected as if we had been in separate places. Mildred, Sam and Charlton were like people in a trance. "I have no words," Mildred said, "for that cathedral." "And the winding cobblestone road to it" —this was Sam—"and the view from it and the interior of it, and that glorious arch over the street." Sophy and I, gabbling to each other about the pleasure of revisiting places seen and loved before, were quelled into silence by the sense of wonder the others could not adequately express.

The telephone call came; we moved to the restaurant, Maxim's. We were welcomed cordially this time by the proprietress and served a meal that justified the wait and my promise of how it would be.

We were at cheese and fruit when Sam lifted his glass.

"This is a special day," he said. "I've waited till now to tell you. It's Mildred's birthday"—he put up a hand for us to let him finish—"and I've got a special present for her."

"Oh, Sam, for heaven's sake," Mildred interjected. "I don't want any presents."

"I know that, but this is a special one. It's Paris."

For the only time since I have known her I saw Mildred shaken. I saw panic in her eyes when she managed to whisper, "Paris?"

Sam nodded vigorously. "Yes sir, Paris. We're not going there to live. I might not pick up the language as fast as I thought and I wouldn't want you to feel you couldn't rely on me. Let's do this trip in France again; it could be even better the second time round"—Sophy and I nodded affirmation to each other—"though I don't see how. But let's keep to the canals."

Mildred's face was transfigured; her eyes were shining, a little mistily; her smile was tremulous. She leaned across the table.

"Play it again, Sam," she said.

L'envoi   1 January 1976

Dear Miss Kimbrough:

Barge news is good news. We had a fine year and although I am now retreating to a vegetable patch in France, everything is set up to keep the *Palinurus* going for another five years at least. The new captain, who also now owns one-half of the *Palinurus,* is Guy Bardet. Do you remember him? He is making some alterations to create more shelf space in the cabins, and to improve the toilets. I enclose the 1976 brochure. The cruises will include Paris to barge and vice versa in our own beautiful little bus, plus one excursion to see more of France. Guy and I will alternate running the boat and driving the bus; that is, he will take over for some cruises and I for others, giving me time off for growing things.

Best regards, and best wishes for your happiness in the New Year,

Richard Parsons

PART TWO

Home Shores:
The "American Eagle"

Chapter 1

Had the brochure come in the mail of my friend the General, we would never have gone on the cruise of the *American Eagle*. The General flouts that kind of reading matter, dropping it unopened into the wastebasket. Animal stories, biography, catalogues and detective fiction make up the list of my favorite reading and I set them down alphabetically because I cannot choose a favorite to head the list. Catalogues of course have a double appeal, the kind that eating Cracker Jack used to have. I say used to have because I have not seen a box of Cracker Jack in years, but in the days when it was delectable to me there was, in addition to the delicious taste of the sugared popcorn, a present at the bottom of the box. Sometimes the present was, in my opinion, a dud. It might be a flat disk with a hole in the center that, put on the tongue and breathed through, made a beautiful piercing whistle. I was not allowed the joy of operating one of these lest I suck it in by mistake and it get stuck in my windpipe.

A catalogue too can produce duds, but there is always the pleasure of its arrival and unwrapping. Among my successes from a catalogue source have been very sharp knives, a pair of red shoes, a wire basket with a handle for turning and drying lettuce, and a device, not unlike a gallows in appearance, for holding and securing the head of a dog while brushing and clipping.

The piece of mail I opened that morning in May did not offer merchandise; its cover was a pen-and-ink drawing of a boat. My nautical vocabulary is both scanty and inaccurate. I do not know when a boat becomes a ship; but this drawing was of a vessel of considerable size, more considerable than the actuality, we discovered. Any catalogue reader knows that a generous allowance must be made for the difference between the illustration and the product.

The name of this greyhound of the sea was revealed in super-capital red letters as the *American Eagle,* and underneath the hull in the illustration, the insignia of an eagle holding in one claw the shield of the United States and in the other what looked like a bundle of arrows. I never learned the significance of these. The caption beneath the eagle read, and it was in red: "American Cruise Line, Inc., Haddam, Connecticut, 06438, telephone (203) 345–8551." For all the comparative modesty of the lettering of "Haddam, Connecticut," those were the words that sparkled for me, because they were familiar.

For those of us who spend our summers within fifty miles of it, Haddam, Connecticut, is the home of the Goodspeed Opera House, and the Goodspeed Opera House is itself a vision of delight, meticulously restored to its original flamboyance; it was built in 1876. We come from a widespread countryside to see the plays presented there during a season that runs from May to October, and some of these have been transferred to Broadway at the close of the Goodspeed season. *Man of La Mancha* began there, and *Shenan-*

186

doah, and this past season *Very Good Eddie.*

By this appraisal, anything coming out of Haddam would be top quality. I opened the brochure with happy anticipation and the very first paragraph was reassuring. "The *American Eagle,*" I read, "is the newest and largest inland cruise ship on the east coast. Measuring over a hundred and fifty feet long, the ship is specifically designed for coastal and inland cruising, providing a level of service unequaled in the trade." It could not have been for me a happier opening. Inland waterways are the lanes I like to follow and I like to be told that even a level of service will be provided. I like to watch sailboats bobbing and dipping, curvetting about on outside waters, and thank God I am not in one of them. But like a duck to water—and ours is the same choice of waters—I will take to river or canal.

I turned the page eagerly to the list of cruises offered. The first one brought the whole pamphlet very close to the brink of the wastepaper basket. "New England Coast Cruise (Eleven Days)," I read. "Anyone who hasn't seen the rugged coast of New England from a boat is missing out —" I do not wish to be on the water side of any coast, and certainly not a rugged one. Edwin Arlington Robinson and I share this conviction, with the difference that he expressed it poetically.

I continued through another coastal offering and came to "Hudson River (Five Days)." My geographic ignorance is on a par with my ignorance of nautical terms, but since I live in New York City and can look across the Hudson River to New Jersey, I knew I could travel on it landlocked against the invasion of a stern and rockbound New England coast.

Actually I had traveled on it at the beginning of the summer I was eight years old, with my parents, my brother Charles, who was two and a half, and my Grandmother Wiles. I had come from Muncie, Indiana, by train to New York. Brother and I had been violently trainsick the whole of the thirty-some-hour journey. We had stayed in New York two days for the recuperation, I daresay, of my parents and grandmother, and had then boarded the *Mary Powell* and traveled to Cornwall-on-Hudson, moved on from there by horse and carriage, another following to bring our luggage, and arrived at a cottage in Upper Cornwall rented for the summer, returning in September via the same route all the way back to Muncie, Indiana. There had been a wide span of years between the *Mary Powell* and the *American Eagle,* but unlike the *Mary Powell,* the Hudson and I had survived, and I was a good deal closer to it than I had been in Muncie, Indiana.

The *American Eagle,* the brochure promised, would go beyond Cornwall all the way to Albany and back again to Haddam, making stops between for passengers to go sight-seeing. Passengers would sleep each night on the boat. This cruise would leave on Sunday the nineteenth of October, returning Friday the twenty-fourth. As in the old hymn "Though every prospect pleases," there was a "though" in this one. Not so lugubrious a one as specified in the hymn —"and only man is vile"—just the proximity of people on a ship that would carry forty-odd passengers.

My only excuse for this isolationist prejudice is that on the other river and canal trips with friends, we have been the only passengers. The boat has been ours, chartered with captain and whatever crew was included in the "package." Once the General and I, in England, hired a boat without crew on the Thames. The General did the navigating and I cast the ropes for mooring and taking off. It was an exhilarating experience but we never repeated it. The knowledge we gained made us realize that for more skillful handling, and less personal recrimination, a professional staff and a larger passenger list would be more restful. These requirements have been justified by the blissful tranquillity of two weeks with friends and crew in France,

England, Ireland, and yet at the time of instigating each of these I had wished it could be in home waters. Friends recruited share my love of Europe by land or river and canal; this was one of the bases of our congeniality. But each time—tiresomely, I daresay—I would assert that someday I was going to offer a prospectus of a boat traveling along our own back or front yard.

I knew about the *Delta Queen,* that plies the Mississippi. However arrogant a New Yorker's conception of the position his metropolis holds in the universe, it does not annex to his property the Mississippi River. Conceding this, I was willing, even eager, to be an explorer, but not in the company of a hundred or so other de Sotos.

This is not an expression of aloofness in my character; age is the deciding factor, and I rejoice in it. "The compensations of age," old or middle, is a phrase I rise to combat with the ferocity of a snapping turtle. "Advantage" is to me the *mot juste* and, like blessings, I count advantages. I do not like tea in the afternoon. I used to pretend I did; I do not drink it any more. I like iced tea with my lunch. I used to be embarrassed to have it in winter; I drink it now every day of the year. I have always abominated a cocktail party; I have not been to one in at least five years. I am, I think, of a gregarious nature, but I am not happy in clumps of people. I have never been on an organized cruise; I must correct that assertion. I *had* never been. Now, with companions of other trips, I have been on the Hudson River cruise of the *American Eagle.*

The opportunity to reaffirm a conviction was a stronger lure than the charm of the route offered. My conviction that had led my friends and me to the fortnight on the *Palinurus* had been, and is, that to some travelers there is double satisfaction in reacquaintance with the familiar combined with the pursuit of the unfamiliar. We of that opinion do not approximate in number those who reach out for the strange and "different," but we were a happy few who had returned to the *Palinurus* only one year ago. The *Palinurus* had been a familiar boat; the waterways we traveled were new to us. The *American Eagle* would be a very new boat, but on these waterways we would be in very familiar surroundings.

Recruiting members for this band of travelers was almost boringly easy; I would have enjoyed the challenge of a little sales resistance. My only turndowns were wails of regret because of other commitments. Mildred and Sam Jaffe had rented for some months a house in Mexico. ("Sam has promised not to *buy,*" Mildred wrote, "and I've made him put it in writing.") Bob Wallsten had to be on hand for publicity requirements because the publication date of his and Elaine Steinbeck's book of John Steinbeck's letters would be during the week of the cruise.

Frances and Albert Hackett accepted immediately—so immediately, Frances told me later, that when she had hung up the telephone, Albert had said to her, "It sounds wonderful, but I didn't catch where Emily said the cruise would be."

Rear Admiral Neill Phillips (ret.), veteran of the first *Palinurus* trip, who had fumed at not being able to make the second, damaged my eardrum in his telephoned reply from Washington.

"Yes! Hell, *yes!* Hurrah for the red, white and blue and the *American Eagle.*"

Charlton's only regret was that Stowe could not come too. "Bad timing for him, wonderful for me. He's off on another documentary that very week, and it was going to be 'mope week' for me. You bet I'll come."

Ellen and Lloyd Garrison, veterans of our cruise in Ireland, were enthusiastic. "Although," Ellen qualified, "I do want to study the brochure."

And the General: "Of course I'm coming. You'd better

give me the maps and charts. I'm not sure you know the East from the Hudson River"—a libelous statement, though I did confuse them once, but that was at the tip of Manhattan, a confusing place. "I'll make a list for the shoe-bag. Gin: Neill drinks martinis; vermouth for the Hacketts and you; Scotch for the Garrisons, Charlton and me. Anyone else coming? You ought to get one new one."

"Got her. Elizabeth Taft."

Sophy's response was as exuberant as I had expected. "Inspired! She knows everybody but the Hacketts, and will they ever take to each other!"

As soon as I had made our reservations and paid a deposit for all of us, I was deluged with pamphlets from East Haddam. I had no sooner distributed them than I had a telephone call from Ellen. She and I were classmates at college; therefore our friendship is of very long standing; therefore I knew she would call me. Ellen and Lloyd are world and widely experienced, travelers. Experience has sharpened Ellen's inherent interest in details. (I remember once telling her about an earthquake I had known at first hand in California: "I was reading in bed when it hit," and she stopped me to ask, "What were you reading?") She has an anticipation of minutiae that would not occur to others, and we are invariably grateful to her in the end.

Her telephone call did hold surprises, because it is impossible to foresee what specifics have demanded Ellen's attention.

"It all sounds lovely," she began. "Great fun and *very* interesting. There *are* a few things I'd like to find out, if you'll call the cruise office. Have you got a pencil? I've made a list.

"One. How many deck chairs can be comfortably set out? Of course we'll want to be outdoors, but if the space is crowded I don't think that would be too comfortable. And if they had to have first and second sittings, like meals on

191

a ship, some people could miss the very things they wanted most to see.

"Two. The brochure says there is a piano in the lounge. Passengers may play on it, but it's also electric, with records or whatever the piano uses. Now, at what time is the piano closed at night? Because if your stateroom is right next to the lounge—and I think that's the one Lloyd and I would take, if no one else wants it—the music could be very disturbing.

"Three. Do we stop at places long enough to leave the boat and do we moor at a dock, so that we can get off? I know it says special tours, but I mean just for walking, because Lloyd has to be able to walk, otherwise he gets awful cramps in his legs, and there certainly isn't enough deck room for him.

"Four. Is there an electric outlet in the staterooms for our electric blankets? We always take them, in a separate duffel bag for each [Ellen is meticulous about her own details]. But we must be sure there's an outlet and the proper voltage, though we do bring a converter for each.

"Five. Will they provide fresh fruit? Sometimes you can only get orange juice. And will they have stewed prunes?

"Six. Are blankets supplied? How many?

"Seven. The pamphlet says liquor is not sold on board. I approve of that. We bring our own. It says 'mixers' will be available at all times without charge. Does that include lemons?"

Frances telephoned again, Albert joining from an upstairs extension:

Frances: "I'm bringing shower caps for everybody, and one bath mat. We'll share that. Albert can take it wherever it's wanted."

Albert: "Anything I can bring? Baking soda, or bluing, maybe?"

The American Cruise Line enclosed, with the receipt for our total payment, which I had collected from the others ($2,320 for eight persons), additional flyers of "Passenger Information." I distributed them. The flyer did not answer Ellen's questions, but it helped.

The program for assembling and boarding on Sunday, October 19, was arranged by the General, and copies sent. It was as follows:

The General, Elizabeth and I would drive together from New York to Watch Hill, Rhode Island. Elizabeth would stay at the cottage she keeps open for her grandchildren; her big house was closed for the winter. Sophy and I would go to the house we jointly own as headquarters for our respective children and grandchildren, some of whom would be there to welcome us. Frances and Albert Hackett would drive with Charlton on Sunday directly from New York to the dock at East Haddam. Ellen and Lloyd, coming from their house in the country at Golden's Bridge, New York, would join us at the dock. Neill Phillips would fly from Washington to Groton, Connecticut, which is not far from Watch Hill. Sophy and I would meet him there on Saturday at 2 P.M. The hour for the rendezvous at the dock would be twelve noon Sunday. We would go a body to the Gelston Hotel across the river and the bridge from the dock. We would lunch there, returning at the specified hour of one-thirty for boarding.

The program did not quite fall into place as outlined. The General's son Denny, his wife, Peggy, and my daughter B. were at the Watch Hill house for a week's holiday. (My daughter's name is Margaret, but she is a twin and her sister is called A.) They telephoned they would like to have friends for dinner Saturday night, a couple and a single man. They hoped that would be agreeable. "They know I'm bringing my cook," was Sophy's comment.

To be ready for the party we drove up on Friday, Elizabeth falling in with this—she is one of the most adaptable people I have ever known. We found our house filled with roses our guests had gathered from Elizabeth's garden at her own injunction to make use of it. Sophy and I were welcomed cordially, Virginia, the cook, extravagantly.

Immediately after early breakfast Saturday morning, Sophy and I prepared to go our separate ways, each of us with a staggering list of chores to be done and food to be bought; the young were going to play tennis. As each of us was stepping into a car, we realized we were setting off in Elizabeth's cars, a station wagon apiece. For Sunday's embarkation with luggage she had ordered them taken out of winter storage at the village garage and delivered to our house. From the chauffeur driven car we had engaged for the trip from New York, we had dropped her off the night before at her cottage. She was now marooned at her cottage with no car. It had been agreed she would come to us for meals except breakfast—and we were more than a mile apart. We rectified this over her protests that she really didn't need a car. Sophy's answer was, "You're such an intelligent woman I can't understand what makes you so docile."

By this time the morning had run on. We combined into one, lists as well as cars; Sophy demurred at my insistence on time out for me to buy a pair of rubber-soled shoes for the boat. (They were crepe-soled jaundice tan, very broad, comfortable, and objects of fun during the whole trip.)

At the meat market we were given a message telephoned from home: the dinner guests would have to bring their two children; the baby-sitter had failed them. With Neill's arrival during the afternoon, this would make twelve. We bought a five-rib roast.

Virginia came out to help us unload the bales of marketing.

"I tried to reach you," she said as she came through the

front door, "but you'd left the market. The people that were coming to dinner telephoned. They said tell you they feel awful, but everything got mixed up—signals crossed, the lady said. Her husband had accepted one invitation and she had accepted another, and they thought they were talking about the same one. They can't any of them come."

The tennis players came back for lunch. Sophy commandeered Denny, and over his protests that it would ruin her beautiful knife, insisted he cut the roast in half. He had to use a wooden mallet to hammer the knife through the bone. The knife was injured and Sophy was reproachful. One severed half was then put in the freezer. We were finishing lunch when I was called to the telephone.

"Darling"—it was Ellen's voice—"the rain is so heavy; it started last night. We're afraid we'll be marooned and can't get out, the stream is already so high. As it is we'll have to take the Jeep to get across. So we're packing like mad and we'll leave right away. Can you put us up for the night?"

With our young in residence and Neill coming, we had no more beds.

"Of course they must come to my cottage," Elizabeth said.

"Denny," his mother requested, "take the half out of the freezer, and tell Virginia to tie it back on. I'll telephone the local help I'd canceled to come after all and help Virginia. I felt unhappy anyway about telling them we didn't need them."

While I went back with Elizabeth to make up beds in the cottage, Sophy left to meet Neill. Denny had offered, *urged* her to let him go, and been asked to lay fires instead; it was getting cold. In spite of heat in the house, it would be pleasant to have the fireplaces going at dinnertime.

It was not only getting cold, it was coming on for a cloudburst that had moved from the Garrisons' milieu to hit us as Sophy reached the airport, almost simultaneously with Neill's plane, which touched ground just as the storm broke. They reported the drive back had been slow and difficult, the road already flooded in low areas, and vision close to zero. Because of this difficulty, the Garrisons did not arrive until after six, and so exhausted they only wanted, they said, a bite and bed.

Extraordinary what a drink, a delicious dinner (tied-together rib roast) and coffee by an open fire will accomplish. We had a late evening of good talk. Ellen and Lloyd left with Elizabeth, Lloyd carrying a dish of prunes that Virginia, learning they were coming, had made for them. The sight of the prunes evidently disturbed Elizabeth, making her feel remiss in hospitality. Asking her guests to wait in the car, she came hurrying back into the house.

From the doorway of the room where we were still sitting around the fire, she said urgently and a little confusedly, "Do you think they'd like a catnip before they go to bed?"

When we had clarified this, I assured her they would not like a nightcap.

Sunday morning it was still raining and the weather forecast was dismal. The Garrisons and Elizabeth arrived from the cottage; we loaded into Elizabeth's two cars, Sophy and Neill leading the way, Elizabeth and I following with Elizabeth at the wheel, and Ellen and Lloyd behind us in their car.

Ellen later chided Elizabeth for driving so slowly. "It's very distracting; it makes your mind wander." I defended Elizabeth: "She was following Sophy." Sophy aggrievedly insisted she had set a modest pace out of consideration for the rest of us. It was quite a rondelay, going full circle a number of times. We reached the parking lot at a few minutes before twelve—eleven forty-seven, the General said—and stepped out into puddles, mud and the sight of the *American Eagle*. Ellen declared it immediately a "darling little house" with some extra things that gave it charm and

distinction. "That deck," she pointed out, "is really a piazza."

In spite of the baggage tags we had been sent, and the note that accompanied them, she still felt incomplete, she said, without a ticket. Did I think perhaps it would be a good idea to go into the office? "There it is right at the dock, and it's so small I'm sure they wouldn't mind your asking if they are *sure* we don't need tickets."

She was appeased by my reminder that I had called the office at her request when the note and tag had come. I had talked with Pat Fitzgerald, the charming girl who had become my telephone pal after a number of calls. Pat had said, "Luggage tags are sufficient. Each one gives your name and cabin number for placement. On this trip," she had added, with an Irish lilt in her voice, "on this kind of a trip, I doubt we'd attract stowaways."

My daughter A. and Bob, a pal, drove into the lot as we were assembling and wondering what to do next. At the sight of Elizabeth, A. broke into laughter so helplessly that for all her apology she could not check it.

"It's those things on your feet," she managed to say. "You always look so stylish, I just couldn't believe it. I'm terribly sorry, really I am." And she was off again.

What with interest in the boat and the whole scene, our attention had not been riveted to Elizabeth's feet, but now the sight was rewarding. Over her shoes she had drawn a pair of garden boots of emerald green rubber but of no shape whatever. Looking down at them herself, reflectively, she said perhaps she had got a size larger than she needed, since they ran so far over the soles of her shoes. She sloshed off to meet Charlton, just driving in with the Hacketts.

In the midst of introductions and explanations—that A. and Bob were not going on the cruise (they had driven over from her house in Branford to have lunch with us and see

198

us off); that Denny, Peggy and B. had sent us off from our own porch, with waves and best wishes (they were leaving shortly to go home, to Boston and Westport, respectively); that the brochure had said cars were to be left in the parking lot for the duration of the cruise and would be protected—some half-dozen young men came from the boat wearing short nylon slickers in orange and yellow, and very attractive to see, both the slicker uniforms and the young men. (They turned out to be college students. Drawn to the otherwise deserted lounge early one morning by the sound of a Bach fugue, Sophy learned, when the pianist had finished, he was a Ph.D. candidate in music, as well as, at the moment, one of the stewards.)

The young men scooped up our luggage, a considerable mound, told us we would find each piece in the proper cabin, and confided we need not take the brochure instructions too seriously. We could stretch the one-thirty boarding to two o'clock.

Elizabeth, Sophy and I, the Goodspeed Opera House regulars, pointed it out to the others, almost directly across the river from our dock, with a long bridge between. Just beyond the theatre, we showed them, across an open square, the charming Victorian hotel, the Gelston, where we would lunch.

Lloyd, immediately announcing his intention of walking there, asked Albert, "Will you walk?"

Albert had not heard the preliminaries to this request and, bewildered, thought Lloyd was asking for a demonstration of his manner of walking. And being by nature an amenable man, he obliged, with a few steps back and forth in front of Lloyd, to the latter's very considerable bewilderment. Once the mutual bafflement was cleared, the two men started off happily, the rest of us following by car. As we paused on the steps of the hotel to wait for the pedestrians and enjoy the charm of the square, we heard a piercing bell ringing insistently, and saw the bridge rise; our companions were on the far side of it.

Ellen was dismayed. "Oh, darling," she reproached me. "You should have warned them this might happen; they could have hurried."

My amazement was as great as her dismay. I had never before seen the bridge lifted in all the years I had been coming here to the theatre. I hadn't even known it was a drawbridge. I learned it twice on the same day. The drawbridge caught the two persistent walkers on our way back from lunch. We had taken literally the assurance of the young men we need not return until two o'clock. It was now two o'clock, and Ellen was waving distractedly to Lloyd, with an open bridge between, calling to him, "Please hurry."

Until she saw the two men coming toward us on the run, Frances had not realized Albert had walked the return trip. "I thought you were in the other car," she told him. "Forgive me for not worrying."

Chapter 2

A. and Bob were allowed on board long enough for a quick survey of the boat, and were loud in their envious approval. Stewards came running to give a message from the captain that if all passengers were on board, and all visitors off, he saw no point in waiting; we would leave now. Sailing time in the brochure was 3 P.M. We left at two-forty by the General's watch, the visitors waving and cheering our departure in ridiculous parody of sailing time for the *Queen Elizabeth.*

Elizabeth and I, rooming together, found our cabin separated from the others by an outside corridor, awash in the rain. Ours was the last one, at the stern; the others clustered toward the bow on either side of the entrance to the lounge.

Like the others, our cabin had its own bath, curtained by a folding screen. The bathroom included a basin, a john and a "telephone" shower—that is, a long flexible metal cord with a handpiece attached, looking not unlike a telephone, to the shower proper. The area for this was a sunken square with center drain. There was no shower curtain, since the shower would be manipulated and directed by hand. It was a thoroughly satisfactory arrangement except that on the first day our shower basin developed a leak that spread water over the whole bathroom floor. To go into the area for any purpose, it was necessary to wear rubber-soled shoes—or Elizabeth's garden boots. She cherishes the memory, she says, of my retirement to the bathroom the first night in the course of preparation for bed, toothbrush in hand, sneakers on my feet, and my nightgown raised, looped around and tucked in at the waist.

The cabin contained two comfortable beds, a narrow aisle between, two chests of drawers, one larger than the other and with a mirror above, a hanging closet, and a large hook on the door, just right, Elizabeth told me with satisfaction, for her belongings, contained, except for a small overnight bag, in a hanging pack. Our two windows, side by side, looked out across the deck to whatever view was beyond.

We made the first survey of our quarters a brief one; we were impatient to join the others for mutual discoveries and appraisals. We found them in full possession of an alcove immediately on the other side of the door from our outside corridor, so immediately my roommate and I were startled by the sight of them as I opened the door, and we were blown in by force of the wind and rain. The alcove had been furnished with a table and a few chairs. Now the tabletop was dotted with books, writing cases and knitting bags, and the number of chairs around it increased from three to nine. Neill had added a rakish touch. He had remembered only at the moment of his departure the note in the flyer that no liquor was obtainable on board. Forgetting about Sophy's shoebag and its contents, he had snatched up a gallon jug a quarter full of gin and, with no time to decant it into a smaller vessel, brought it in hand and offered it on the table for general consumption. Elizabeth is an indefatigable photographer; her camera is as indispensable an accessory as her handbag. She promptly photographed this scene. In that picture the most conspicuous accessories are Neill's jug of gin and one of the books I had brought, written by a good friend, Robert Thomsen: *Bill W.,* the biography of the founder of Alcoholics Anonymous.The rain continued steadily as we made our way down the Connecticut River; even so, it was a lovely ride, we said. We saw charming houses set back with trees on either side; directly in front, sloping lawns down to the water's edge. These houses were visible only from the water; from the roadside they were planted out. The foliage, even in the rain, had color.

Sometime after four, we came out of the Connecticut River and into Long Island Sound. The General did not give us the exact time of this confluence, because she was preoccupied and a little apprehensive, though she was reluctant to admit she does not like rough water. There was unmistakably a marked difference in our smoothness of passage. Neill said we were in luck because the wind was behind us; we were not bucking it.

"Call it whatever you like," the General told him. "It's motion. I call it rough."

The General was distracted and we were all of us dismayed by a reminder from Charlton that on the authority of the brochure, dinner would be at six o'clock. We rushed into action. Sophy brought the shoebag from the cabin she and Charlton occupied; others, scattering and on the double, brought from the lounge plastic glasses, bowls of ice out of an ice machine, sliced lemons, olives, cheese, crackers and nuts, all of these supplied without charge.

The dining room was below, down a flight of steep, al-

most precipitous, stairs. Though it was not on Ellen's list, I had requested in advance a table reserved throughout the cruise for our band. All the tables, we saw, were long, accommodating at least as many guests as we numbered. Frances was reassured by this. She had been afraid, she said, we would give an appearance of special privileges. I forbore to mention the nook we had appropriated, without even requesting it.

We dined well; the food was delicious and attractively presented—arranged, not heaped on platters, enticingly garnished. We served ourselves from the platters and vegetable dishes, and the vegetables, a real test of a sophisticated menu and its preparation, were, like the little bear's porridge, I said, just right: not soggy or overcooked, they had texture as well as flavor. As we left the dining room I pointed out to Ellen large bowls of fruit on a table down the center of the room. She took an apple for herself and one for Lloyd.

After dinner, returning to our nook, we found everything we had left, untouched, though Sophy had returned the shoebag to her cabin, together with Neill's jug. The Hacketts, Sophy and I played Scrabble at the table; the others went into the lounge to read, but none of these activities were uninterrupted. We were so astonished to find it still early twilight after dinner—the habitual hour for each of us was seven or half past—we were constantly interrupting, urging one another of our group to watch the changing scene as the dusk came on and lights came out along the shore. To be moving at this time of day or evening was a new experience for us, even though each of us had gone abroad by ship. On a barge, travel stops in the late afternoon, because the locks are closed. Now, in the evening, we were not moving across an ocean, nor had we moored. We were passing houses and people, along a shore we had traveled many times by car.

"Lawk-a-mercy," I said as I started for bed, "I really don't know where I'm at."

When the reservations had been made, Elizabeth and I had suggested to each other that we room together. "Anyone who has gone to boarding school can share a room and not be in the least disturbed by it," she had maintained, and I heartily supported this point of view. On the *American Eagle* there are no single cabins. For single occupancy, double fare is required, an unappealing qualification, we thought.

Neill accepted double fare and single occupancy. "I'm a big man," he said, "and I like to spread."

As we started the going-to-bed pattern, my roommate and I talked about and agreed on the overall one we would follow:

Each of us had an eyeshade, and was accustomed to using it. If one wanted to read and the other was ready for sleep, the shade would be applied. In the morning I would precede her; she is not an early riser and I am. She was disconcerted to remember that breakfast was served only from eight to nine, relieved to call to mind later that coffee from a machine, and rolls or "Danish," would be available in the lounge at any time. If she chose to skip the breakfast hour she need not fast. By this single-file dressing process we would avoid buttock-to-buttock encounters.

The design offered, modified, amplified and accepted, we turned out our bed lights almost simultaneously. No pattern had been set for sleeping; mine was a broken one. I was wearing a pale blue voluminous nightgown, a Christmas present I had not worn until I could show it off. Elizabeth's comments had been highly satisfactory. Sometime after the first deep sleep, always the most delicious, I woke with a feeling of dampness somewhere about my knees. I thought I had probably not dried off sufficiently the outside of the hot-water bottle I always take to bed. I did not want to rouse enough to go into the bathroom to dry it off more thoroughly; I drifted off again. The next time I woke it was because the dampness seemed to have increased. I did not want to wake Elizabeth, but I felt a necessity to investigate. With the bottle held away from me, I got out of bed as noiselessly as possible, went into the bathroom, closed the folding screen behind me, turned on the light and upended over the basin the hot-water bottle at the very moment it split all the way down the center from an initial split as long as my forefinger.

For extra warmth I had also attached my heating pad. Since the outlet was beyond the foot of my bed, on the far side of the door, beside one of the chests of drawers, the cord—I had not brought an extension—came across the door and just inside the foot of my bed; I had reasoned neither of us would be inclined to go out on deck during the night. I had lifted the bedding at the foot and slipped the pad in, providing warmth for my feet, though I could not move the pad farther up lest I pull out the plug. Happily the flood had not extended to it; I daresay I might have been electrocuted. I felt my way back to the towel rack, brought a bath towel, spread it on the bed, put my hands along to smooth it, and found it already soaking wet. So I stripped the bed, put the blankets over the mattress—only a little damp—rolled myself in and passed the rest of the night in dreamless sleep.

Waking the next morning, I looked across at Elizabeth, who had not stirred during all my maneuvers. She had not taken off her night eyeshade; I could have made my rearrangements with the lights full on. I did not wear the voluminous nightgown again, and thanked heaven I had brought two, because the blue one, at the end of the cruise, had still not dried completely.

At breakfast I found the others already at our table—I had been delayed by explanations to my horrified roommate. One look at what was on the table and I yielded to a disgraceful craving I have since had to discipline, though I have occasional reminiscent dreams of: platters of fried eggs, piping hot and not a trace of grease, surrounded by strips of crisp bacon. There was toast in a basket, pats of butter in shallow bowls, and a wide selection of jams and marmalade. I did draw the line at waffles with maple syrup, offered as a second course, and my sense of guilt at what I had already savored was a little assuaged by the sight of some of my companions moving, and seemingly without a qualm, into the second course. They had, of course, had orange juice or another fruit as preface to the eggs and bacon.

Conversation was, understandably, desultory, but I did learn, to my considerable surprise, we had not docked the previous night until half-past ten or a little later; the long day had sent us all to bed an hour before. Our port had been City Island, but arriving there, our captain had discovered, to his discomfiture, the berth reserved for the *American Eagle* had been usurped; we had been forced to drop anchor outside. We had therefore turned, circled, moved throughout the night, to the sound of clanking anchor chains. The General's comment on my obvious surprise: "Evidently *nothing* disturbed you." I let that pass.

As I left the dining room, Albert was behind me. When I turned back, apologizing that I hadn't realized he was talking to me, he reddened a little.

"Actually I was trying nautical phrases over to myself, but I haven't got this right: 'I'm going aboveboard.' "

I told him to try again and we went upstairs together.

The weather was still intermittently rainy but the rain was so light we went on deck to watch a wider vista than the large window by our nook provided. We were about to emerge into the East River and progress down the whole length of Manhattan. At first we were speechless at the impact of that dramatic skyline; when we did speak we betrayed an embarrassing disorientation. Our rate of speed contributed to our confusion. On the barge trips, we had known only its own speed in that countryside, but now we were moving at a slow pace through territory we were accustomed to cover frequently by car. When I fumed at having missed a sight of the UN building from the river, I discovered it looming into my vision some twenty minutes later. I have traveled purposefully the length of Manhattan in order to show it to overseas visitors, but I have never shown or seen it from a boat, and consequently never been so aware of its length.

Rounding the tip of Manhattan, I did reveal my momentary confusion between the East and the Hudson rivers. It was brought about, I shall always maintain, by my wonder and joy at the sight of the Brooklyn and other bridges from below. I had not seen nor been aware of the delicate tracery, the almost gossamer quality, of their underpatterns. And then the Statue of Liberty. I suspect there are those with souls so dead their hearts do not skip a beat nor their breaths catch in their throats at the sight of that figure, but thank God I am not one of them. Then we were identifying, often mistakenly, familiar places on the West Side. We were not mistaken in our identification of the George Washington Bridge, but garrulous in our admiration of its truly exquisite underpinning.

When I thought we must be approaching West Point I read a sign: SNEDENS LANDING. Confused as I was about relative distances by land and water, I did know something about Snedens Landing, thanks to Nancy Hamilton and other friends who have lived there and cherish its history. It was originally, they had told me, Captain Sneden's Landing for Captain Dobbs' Ferry. Through the years "Captain" has been dropped and the spelling become erratic, sometimes with two e's and other variations. Repeating this bit of lore to my friends, I added the information that my nephew Charles Kimbrough lived with his family directly across, at Dobbs Ferry. When he was playing in the theatre in New York he commuted easily to and from performances, and I, going to lunch with them at their house, had found the trip shorter than to friends in lower Manhattan.

Then we passed a series of beautiful and quite imposing places, set back from broad lawns and half-encircled by magnificent trees. Neill identified the one-time Vanderbilt and other houses, and we knew we were in Dutchess County around Rhinebeck.

Chapter 3

We reached and docked at West Point in late afternoon. The dock lay alongside a railroad track, abandoned now for passenger traffic, but very active for transporting freight. We agreed it was a commentary on the age to which we had come that the sound of a train whistle and the sight of headlights as we heard and saw them that night, a line of cars behind, brought back such nostalgia we were children again, down at the depot to watch the trains go by.

A bus was waiting for us at the landing, the chauffeur an articulate, well-informed guide and an expert driver. I am, I admit, a craven in a car, and the road ahead of us looked to me a perilous upgrade. After the first bend, I relaxed; the driver will never have a better commendation.

The drive was rewarding. The main chapel and its stained-glass windows are beautiful, each of these a parting gift from a graduating class. The small chapel beside the cemetery is of quite different character, and deeply moving. Weddings can be held there, our guide told us, and burial services conducted. Around the walls of the interior, plaques like small wooden shields record the names of West Point men who fought and died in the Revolutionary War. We saw familiar names of history—Anthony Wayne, Artemas Ward, Philip Schuyler, John Cadwalader and more. We came upon one that bore only the rank and date of birth, "Major-General, 1740," and had to learn from our driver-guide this one was for Benedict Arnold, who had been commandant of the fort at West Point before he turned traitor. Albert told us he had seen at Westminster Abbey the burial place of Benedict Arnold, with an inscription to a great war hero of England. The chapel itself is small and whitewashed inside, with only the dark wood of the shields for contrast.

A little beyond the chapel the driver pointed out to us a memorial shaft to one Margaret Corbin. This was in recognition of her fighting valor. Standing at the side of her husband when he fell, she had promptly taken his place at the cannon and continued to fire.

"You probably know her," the driver said, "as Molly Pitcher. The reason for the difference in names is that during the Revolutionary War the women often accompanied their husbands to the front, took care of men about them when they became wounded, and above all provided water. For this reason the women were always known as Molly Pitchers."

The view from the lookout point is one of the most impressive panoramas I have ever seen, encompassing the sweep of the quiet river, the gentle hills beyond, all a blaze of autumn foliage in the afternoon sun, a grim paradox of the purpose of the place. If ever a landscape conveyed tranquillity, majesty, serenity and peace this one was its embodiment. That this lovely spot should be the shaping ground for specialists in war seems bitterly ironic. It would somehow be more appropriate, I thought, for a great military center to be in a bleak, forbidding landscape of rocks, jagged crags and barren hills.

One aspect of the vast complex, encompassing fifteen thousand acres, we were told, was strange. We pointed out, but did not ask our driver the reason for, the absence of activity and the scant number of people we saw. We found out the reason the next day.

Not far from our boat, we came to the little village of West Point. It is so small and so self-effacing at the foot of the overwhelming crest it is like a child hiding behind its mother's skirts. Our driver stopped at a kind of newstand-cum-drugstore.

"Postcards," Albert and Frances called to each other, and were the first off the bus.

At the shoebag hour that evening we reviewed the day and its culmination, its physical summit at West Point. But where, we said, were the cadets, those beautiful young men in their beautiful uniforms? Elizabeth, looking off dreamily into the nowhere, said, "I was in uniform once," and wished with all her heart, she said later, she had never voiced that reflection, because we gave her no peace until she had told us the circumstances.

"It was during the First World War. With dogged persistence I had worn down my father to permission to come from Detroit, my native heath, to New York. I was enrolled at the School of Philanthropy, as it was called then"—of all things. Now it's the New York School of Social Work. "I was very young and, I suppose, very docile."

"Just what I've said about you," Sophy interpolated. "But go on."

Elizabeth continued. "I had a good friend who was very affirmative, if you know what I mean. She said young women should take an active part in the war, not just roll bandages and such. We were young, vigorous, athletic—I was not in the least athletic—we must be trained for an

213

active part. Somehow she organized her friends and part of the army—at least she persuaded the army to allot an officer to train us. He was terribly handsome." She lapsed into dreaminess again.

The General pulled her up sharply. "Go on," she said sharply, and Elizabeth obliged.

"My friend—her name was Elizabeth too—said we must have proper military uniforms and sent us to a tailor, who turned out to be one of the most expensive in New York. I had to borrow from my mother two months' advance allowance to pay for mine, but they really were terribly smart. We wore puttees, of course, very well fitted, but the trousers were the showpiece, you might say. They sort of ballooned out just below the hips and then tapered down. The jacket was very well cut too, and under that we wore a tailored shirt with collar and tie." She broke off, rocking her head between her hands. "Oh, why did I ever get into this, the awful thing that happened! Mercifully I'd forgotten it—all those years ago."

A chorus told her she could *not* stop now. Taking a deep breath, she continued.

"Well, all right. We had regular drills at the armory—you know, at Sixty-sixth Street and Park Avenue—under the command of that handsome captain. One day we were marching round and round, doing turns and about-faces, and a shoulder strap of my underwear dropped down. You know how uncomfortable that is. So I did what every woman in the world does automatically; I reached under my snappy uniform shirt and pulled it up. And that captain *bellowed* at me: 'Sergeant Clark. Keep your hands on the seams of your trousers.'"

She was, of course, from that moment, Sergeant, sometimes Sarge, to us.

We were still enjoying Elizabeth's new title when we separated for more excursions into West Point next day.

We had wakened to a startling and lovely change in the weather. What to wear? I had come on board Sunday wearing a suit, and over it a topcoat. On Monday morning I had been thankful I had brought a nylon windbreaker with a fleece lining. Monday afternoon I had shed the windbreaker, replaced it with a light topcoat, and later shed that. Tuesday's outer gear, I decided, would be a sweater.

Immediately after lunch, Albert, Sophy, Charlton and I walked up the road to the broad area the buildings' circle, and what a difference from the overall atmosphere of the day before. We had scarcely started our climb—and it is not actually that; the slope is gentle but continuous for a considerable distance, winding around and up—when we began encountering runners, not joggers, in white shorts and yellow jumpers. Each of them without breaking step or breath would greet us: "How do you do?" or "Hi!" or "Hello." When to our astonishment we recognized one who had passed us and gone down to the bottom of the hill and was now passing us on his ascent, we ventured more than an answering hello.

"How many times have you done this?" I asked.

"Five," was his answer, "and I have six more to go."

"Are you on a team?" Sophy called, and the answer floated back to her.

"Yes, a marathon team."

Charlton, not for him to hear, said, "Would you mind looking at the muscles of his legs?" They were like the arm muscles of a strong man at the circus when he bends his elbow and deliberately inflates them. Albert did not share our admiration. "That boy's not doing it for pleasure," he pronounced darkly. "He's doing penance for something." Because of a strict Catholic background, Albert tends to give a melancholy interpretation to strenuous activity except when practiced by a team.

As we rounded the last curve we came upon team upon

team and squad upon squad on an enormous playing field. This was evidently football practice. Meantime and continuously we saw the runners up and down the road, until my prophecy was that I would see in my sleep an unending stream of young men running. Obviously our timing the afternoon before had been during the academic period, when the cadet body was confined indoors. I do not know why we had not seen other people about. Now there were women with children and men obviously above the age of the cadets. We stopped one very young woman with a child to ask the way to the chapels; I wanted the others to see the stained-glass windows of the one and the charming simplicity of the other, with its touching shields. The young woman told us it was too far to walk and directed us to retrace our steps a hundred yards or so, cross the road and we would see a flight of stairs down, and at the foot what she called "the bubble."

We followed her instructions and came to a glass-enclosed shelter open on one side, the waiting place for "the shuttle." That is a constant bus service around the whole post; and, to Sophy's such rapturous delight that she repeated the happy news over and over, there was no charge. The driver was an affable Negro who explained his run did not go near the chapel but did stop by the cemetery if we wished to get out there; that he would go on to the end of the line, the post exchange. This was his last run of the day, but there would be another shuttle to take us back. The one we rode passed many of the places we had seen the day before, and other roads we had not seen. West Point had become now a community, almost like any other —women, children boarding and leaving the bus, children running for it carrying their knapsacks—but there was one unmistakable difference. When cadets boarded and left the bus, each one thanked the driver and was in turn answered courteously. On our return, members of a juvenile football team boarded the bus, all in their uniforms with absurdly padded shoulders on such slight little figures. There was considerable shouting back and forth and tumult, a kind of incongruity amidst all the military surroundings. An even greater one to me was the sight of a young officer in uniform; I could not see the insignia that marked his rank but he was young. He carried in one hand a briefcase and on the other arm a baby about a year old. Such evidence of domesticity had a special flavor in those surroundings.

We left the bus, being careful to thank the driver, at a point different from that of our departure, because Sophy remembered this as part of her before-breakfast walk that morning. She led us across the road, and we were suddenly underneath buildings, with a stone arch overhead and labyrinthine passages leading away from us. We seemed to be under a compound of at least two, possibly four, units. Suddenly it was as if we were in a medieval castle; we might almost have come out at a moat and a drawbridge. Curiously, the structure of gray stone reminded Sophy and me simultaneously of the one-time garrison, now a museum, at Athlone in Ireland.

We emerged on the road again at the head of another roadway sloping gently downhill, and within a short distance caught sight of our own little ship below.

As we came near we saw what was obviously a ferryboat, a diminutive one, pulling out and heading up and across the river. I do not know its destination, and though I had a moment's inclination to ask, it was short-lived because there was something that pleased me about the sight of this small vessel, with some lights twinkling on it, heading out to what seemed to be only thick woods, its destination unknown.

Chapter 4

During our shoebag hour Tuesday night we were told by the purser we would not go so far as Albany, that the next day we would proceed some distance, not determined, farther up the Hudson would then turn back, spend the night in West Point again and on the following day go to New York, because the captain had information he could have a berth at the South Street Seaport, where there was a museum, and there would be other points of interest.

Our group was indignant and told the purser so emphatically. He was so courteous and gentle we were apologetic about inflicting our indignation on him, but we did wish to convey we thought it irresponsible to change the route that had been set out in the brochure, and that had included reaching Albany, where there were places—in and beyond the city—we wanted very much to see. Sophy particularly had wanted to visit the new buildings of the state university at Albany. We made it clear had there been untoward circumstances, any kind of delay or accident, that prevented our reaching the announced destination, we would have been not only reconciled but understanding; but to have this quixotic change of plan thrust on us was, besides being a sort of irresponsibility, a disregard of the passengers' trust in the carrying out of the trip for which they had engaged passage.

Since then I have apologized. How mistaken I was to have objected! The stay in New York was one of the most fascinating interludes of the entire trip. What my friends and I had not taken into consideration, because we were annoyed, was that to many of the other passengers this was an opportunity to see a city they had never set foot in. Our stewardesses were like children suddenly told they were going to the circus; later we became almost as wide-eyed. We were introduced to a part of the city we had never seen; more than merely a strange metropolis, it was like another country, and we reveled in it.

The South Street Seaport comprises a wide area of landmarks, many of them in process of restoration. Ellen and Lloyd were the only ones of our group who knew about it. To our chagrin, we overheard other passengers displaying considerable knowledge in their anticipation of actually visiting it. In all too small atonement for my ignorance of this complex, I made a vow to tell other New Yorkers to make a pilgrimage there; the going is easy by subway or bus. Once there, they will be given, at the museum, a chart of places to visit: ships and boats, a blacksmith's shop, a model shop and gallery, many restaurants and the museum itself. Ellen and Lloyd did not meet any of our group there at the moment they visited the blacksmith's shop, but they did see and chat with a friend, an architect, who was ordering specially made wrought-iron work.

On the morning of our detour to New York, I was dressing, and talking again to Elizabeth in her berth about my irritation at this deflection from the specified course. Suddenly the boat seemed to go berserk. There was a sort of grinding noise and a momentary jolt. I was sent off balance, to make an arch over my cabinmate, my hands against the wall on the far side.

"I've gone aground twice before," she said calmly. "This is the third time."

Shouts and running footsteps along our outside corridor pulled me upright and out the door in time to see, just off our bow on my right, the head of a deer that was swimming across the river. We had deferred to his right of way. Later

that morning I'had a talk with the purser; I was already beginning to apologise; perhaps the beautiful sight of the deer had had a mellowing effect.

The purser's name, I learned, is Alfred H. Gabriels and he comes from Essex, Connecticut. I learned this much when I invited him to join me in our nook. I was its only occupant at the moment, and Mr. Gabriels had approached to say again he hoped the detour would not put us off the whole cruise and even the *American Eagle.* This was when I began to feel uncomfortable, and to ask questions.

Mr. Gabriels' function on the boat, I learned, is like that of a hotel manager. He handles the ship's books, oversees the purchase and storage of all supplies. He sees that navigational charts, tide and current tables are up to date, and is the liaison between passengers and staff. He was coaxed out of retirement after more than one hundred transatlantic crossings on large passenger ships.

The crew members, Mr. Gabriels told me, come for the most part from the area in and around Haddam and Essex. Some of the girls had worked before as waitresses, but none of them had had experience on a ship. I interrupted to assure him we had found it an unusual group, efficient, quick, charming and eager to serve. Mr. Gabriels was pleased. The engineer, he said, was of "genius category." He had graduated from the Maritime Academy at the end of three years. This had not happened before. A degree was customarily achieved—and with great difficulty—at the end of four years.

Captain Thorp is a man from Maine. "He's spent a good part of his life on and around boats," Mr. Gabriels said. "He's been very much a part of this one from the first drawings."

The personnel work in shifts of three trips on and then one trip off. The captain himself has an alternate, and so does the chef.

Lloyd joined us unexpectedly, dropping into a chair beside me and wiping his forehead with a handkerchief he pulled from the pocket of his raincoat. He apologised for interrupting our conversation, but explained this was an emergency, a grave emergency. He had lost a muffler—not any muffler, Ellen had pointed out, but a very beautiful and expensive cashmere muffler. Overcome, then, not only by a sense of loss, but by guilt, he had searched everywhere.

"I assure you there's not a corner of our cabin untouched. I've turned up everything, including the mattresses. I've reported the loss; I've gone over the whole lounge; turned up everything there too."

No wonder, I told him, he had had to wipe his forehead after all that exertion. Wouldn't he relax at least for a moment, and take off his coat?

He accepted the suggestion gratefully and took off his coat. The muffler was extended the inside length of one sleeve.

The coat itself had been the instigation of the crisis. Almost at the hour of departure from East Haddam, Ellen had noticed how conspicuously Lloyd was shaking with cold in the rain. She had then discovered that though he had brought his raincoat, he had failed to insert the fleece lining. Lloyd is widely recognized as a distinguished lawyer and champion of civil rights. The list of his federal, academic and municipal appointments is very long. In his broad range of activity, he tends to overlook small things.

That our stopover in New York was unexpected was evidenced by the improvised landing on which we reached the dock. At each of the other stops we had come directly to dockside from the lower deck, the location of the dining room, with a very short span between. At this pier we came from our cabin and lounge deck, onto a large solid block of wood, like an enormous chest, about three feet high. Our gangplank was laid flat across this, the indented steps down which we had gone now stretching flat across the chest. At the far end of this platform other steps had been salvaged from somewhere. They were quite rough and very steep. One of the stewards was in constant service giving a hand to ascending and descending passengers, since there was no side rail.

Along the length of the pier we saw rows of metal benches, all of them occupied; there were people standing about; others had brought and were using folding chairs. These spectators looked to be young business men and women; many of them had brought their lunches, many were leaning back on the seats, eyes closed, sunning them-

selves. There was a delicious breeze, but a giant thermome-
ter on a building nearby registered the temperature: 73
degrees.

Obviously our arrival was as great a surprise to the sun-
bathers as the sight of them was to us, but the American
Cruise Line was evidently prepared for any opportunity to
make itself known. A large carton filled with brochures,
familiar to us, appeared at the side of the steward on gangplank duty, and his duty was extended to distributing them.
In no time at all they were being perused and talked about,
the readers pointing out to one another locations on the
actual boat, as they were illustrated.

On one side of our dock we saw a floating hospital, as it
was identified in large letters across its side. During the
summer months the Floating Hospital carried convales-
cents for a day's outing on the river around Manhattan.
There were no passengers, only a skeleton staff of some
sort, but through the windows along the deck we could see
rows of baby cribs, and we were aware that the approach
to the deck of the ship was by way of a long sloping ramp.
Obviously the passengers would not walk up any steps.

On the other side of the dock were two small sailing
ships. One, we learned, had come from Denmark; the
other, from Poland, was on its way around the world on a
scientific expedition, taking samples of water everywhere
for signs of pollution. I talked to one of the Polish officers,
who spoke French. They had been in Greenland, where
they had been blocked by ice in their passage north, and
had had to turn back. On the deck of this little vessel there
was a dogsled. We saw freighters bearing the flags and
names of such far-off places as Monrovia and even China.

Immediately after lunch people left our ship and scattered in every direction. Returning, Sophy and Charlton
said they had been to a cocoa exchange, exciting to see and
hear. The participants seemed to be mostly South Ameri-

cans, the babel was deafening—bidding, shouting to one another—and over it the voice of the auctioneer, then one of the officials, calling off the approaching deadline, three o'clock. As it became five minutes, four minutes and so forth, they said the bidding grew more hysterically impassioned. At the stroke of three and the clang of a bell, total silence. I will make a special visit to this someday.

It was an eerie feeling actually to be in New York and yet not part of it. We had talked among ourselves in the morning about how reasonable it would be to go uptown, have lunch, look at our mail and return again; somehow the prospect did not appeal to us. However, Charlton decided that because there was heavy committee work ahead for her, and Stowe might, he had said, get home that day, she would end her trip there. She telephoned her apartment from the dock and, to their mutual astonishment, Stowe answered; he had just got home an hour before. He said, not expecting her, he was having a meeting at the apartment for the music settlement in which he is deeply involved and would be finished at eight o'clock. Why did he not come down for her then? She said she was delighted at this suggestion; so were we all, hearing it. We would ask in the dining room to have some dinner saved for him that he could eat when he arrived.

Elizabeth also went on the dock, telephoned dear friends, Minnie and Hunter Marston, told them to their utter amazement where we were. They said they would come down in their car to pay us a visit and should arrive at about four o'clock. Sophy, Elizabeth and I would meet them at the entrance to our pier.

The dock was a very long one and when they arrived it was impossible for Minnie, who has arthritis, to walk that long distance; yet she was eager to see the boat at close hand. There were benches all along the dock so that she could sit comfortably, but how in the world to transport her to a closer view? Suddenly it occurred to me that a hospital ship must have a wheelchair.

I had been talking to her at the street end of the dock and I said, "Wait a few minutes; let me see if I can find something."

I went back to the hospital ship, Hunter with me, and hallooed from the foot of their gangplank, because there was a chain across it with the sign NO ADMITTANCE.

Two young men came out on deck; one spoke very little English, a Puerto Rican, I think, and the other from his accent was a native-born American.

I said, "Would it be possible for us to borrow a wheelchair? We have a friend who cannot walk the distance."

Obviously such a request had never been made to them before; they looked at each other inquiringly and one of them said, "How long?"

My answer was, "Not more than half an hour and you can keep an eye on us the whole time."

So the Puerto Rican, shrugging his shoulders, said, "Why not? Just a minute," and presently came back with what looked like a brand-new wheelchair.

He brought it to us, verifying what I had surmised was the purpose of the ramp. It did not go straight up, but curved much like the road at West Point, this of course to enable attendants to push more readily the wheelchairs of the patients who were to be taken on the ship. We thanked the attendant and Hunter gave him five dollars, which he refused to take, until I said, "Please, buy a little treat for your patients. We are very grateful."

We took the wheelchair back to Minnie. Hunter and I pushed her the length of the dock over the rough boards that made its flooring. Wonderful sport that she is at eighty-eight, she held each arm of the chair and declared the going was very healthful—like jogging. We pulled up at the foot of our gangplank so that we could point out every detail within sight, and she could see some of the passengers moving about on deck and inside. She wanted to know about them, pointing to individuals. Where did they come from, what did they do? We had to admit, shamefaced, we had scarcely talked to anybody. She was incredulous.

"We have such a good time in our own group," I said defensively.

Minnie said nothing, but Hunter spoke.

"Minnie would have talked to at least a quarter of the passengers before she went to bed the first night." I'm sure she would.

Hunter asked us to go to dinner with them. Minnie broke in on our rather halting regrets and excuses.

"I wouldn't think of it if I were you. You'd break the spell. This is something quite different and I think you ought to stay with it."

That was exactly the way we had talked earlier among ourselves; Minnie is a perceptive woman.

Before dinner a message was posted at the head of the bizarre exit asking passengers who came in after eight o'clock to use the "main gate," and we were not sure which or what this was. Obviously it was an improvisation like the landing device, because at no other landing would there have been the slightest provocation to be on the town after eight o'clock.

As a matter of fact, we were surprised to find almost the full complement. Our surmise was they were taking advantage of the meal included in the price of the trip and were going to sally afterward. We were mistaken. We learned. To the amazement of others, we had gone to bed the night before during a game in the World Series. It had ended in a tie between the Cardinals and the Red Sox. Almost the whole passenger list had assembled in the lounge to watch it. No one had been aware of the absence of members of our group. Lloyd, Albert, Neill and Charlton had not only sat up but participated in the game, with cheers, groans and occasional eccentric dance steps. Neill, who, it turned out, had come to know a surprising number of the audience, had officiated as a sort of chairman and arbiter among factions.

Therefore, on the night that might have been spent on the town, most of our fellow passengers gathered to watch the grand finale.

Stowe arrived at about half-past eight, to be welcomed with a dinner of flounder stuffed with crab meat and accessories. He enjoyed it with relish, heightened by a glass of wine, courtesy of Frances and Albert, who had brought on board a case to supplement the shoebag provisions.

Finished, complete with a lethally rich dessert, Stowe announced he thought it a pity to go all the way back uptown, thereby missing part of the ball game. He settled in the lounge with Charlton, the other participants and chairman Neill Phillips.

The preceding night, before the end of the game, Neill, sleepy, had relinquished his post to a far from impartial spectator, who was lavishly courting bets against his partisanship of Cincinnati, not because of conviction, he admitted later, but to "stir things up."

Albert, too, had not stayed through the game, retiring reluctantly only because too much TV habitually brought on a headache. Lloyd, compassionate over Albert's reluctant withdrawal, at dramatic moments had rushed to the Hacketts' cabin, flung open the door and bawled into the darkness the score or the drama of the moment. When a light was unexpectedly turned on in the corridor he had remembered belatedly the cabin held another occupant: he saw Frances asleep with the sheet over her head.

That had been the night before Stowe's visit. For the final game the spectators comprised almost the full passenger list. That game was an even stronger magnet than night life in New York. When I said good night to Charlton, who would not be with us the next day, I knew I would not forget the sight of that rapt audience and the incongruity of Charlton and Stowe among its members on the *American Eagle* at South Street Seaport, preferred to their own living room on Seventy-third Street. Before I opened my cabin door I enjoyed an incongruity of my own. Standing at the railing of our outside corridor, I watched the magic of the lights of New York at night from a part of the city I had never seen before.

Next day I learned the passenger who had made bets to "stir things up" had collected a hatful of winnings.

New York was the climax of the trip. On Thursday, our last day, I repeated my vows of conversion to New York as port of call. At about four o'clock we docked at

Greenport, Long Island. On the trip out we had been in closer view of the Connecticut shore; this time we had been nearer Long Island. Returning to our base at the shoebag hour, we brought back a unanimous opinion that the village was a charming and picturesque center for fishermen, but by the number of art, gift and sports shops, it was also frequented, probably crowded, by summer visitors. We had come at exactly the right time; we seemed to be the only tourists.

On Friday morning at ten o'clock or thereabouts (the General did not verify this), we came down the gangplank at East Haddam.

"Look over there, Albert," I heard Lloyd say. "The bridge is up again."

Neill, carrying his gallon jug, waved it toward the river. "I hadn't realised before how lovely the opera house is from here."

Ellen stopped at the foot of the gangplank to look back. "You see? Now the deck from here is a piazza again. Isn't it charming!"

As in "The Hunting of the Snark":

I have said it twice . . . I have said it thrice:/What I tell you three times is true.

There is more in second sights than first meets the eye.

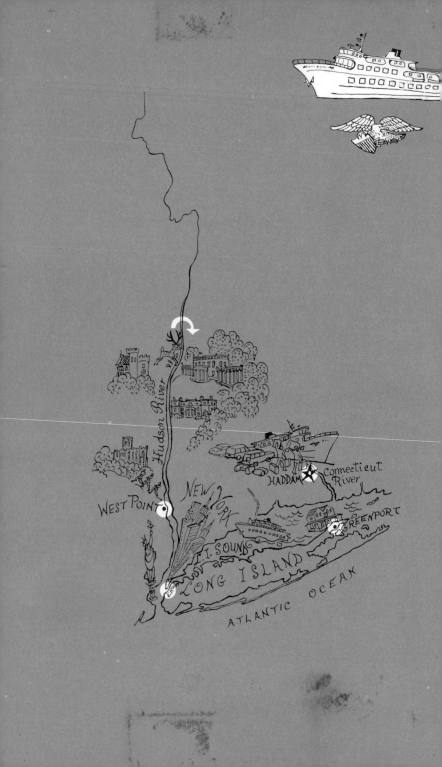